Dividends Book

The Secret to Retire Rich

John Kleemann

Copyright © 2014 John Kleemann
All rights reserved.

ISBN: 1494975742
ISBN 13: 9781494975746

Contents

Disclaimer	ix
Summary	xi
The Power of Dividend Income Revealed, and How You Can Apply It RIGHT NOW to Your Own Financial Situation!	xi
What Are YOU Doing About YOUR Future Financial Plans?	xii
Pragmatic, Down to Earth, Actionable Information!	xii
Three Crucial Factors	xiii
Financial Heresy Exposed	xv
Inconceivable, Unimaginable Debt	xv
The Dividends Book in Action!	xix
Introduction	xxi
Chapter 1—The Millionaire's Secret	1
The Power of Compound Dividends	3
The Rolling Snowball	3
Ideal for Long-Term Investors	4
The Rule of 72	5
Dividend Growth with Compounding	6
Dividend Reinvestment Plans (DRIPs)	7
Applying the Rule of 72 on DRIPs	7

Chapter 2—The DRIP   9

Dividend Reinvestment Plan (DRIP) – Investor's Benefits   12
DRIP – Joining the Plan   13
Why DRIP?   15

Chapter 3—Roth IRA versus Traditional IRA   19

Traditional IRA   21
Roth IRA   21
SEP IRA   22
Roth IRA – The Larger Picture   22
How is Roth IRA Different?   22
Roth IRA Investment Options   24
Calculating Roth IRA Gains   24
Eligibility for Roth IRA   25
Traditional IRA – The Larger Picture   26
A Major Disadvantage of Traditional IRA   26
Places to Establish Traditional IRA   27
Roth vs. Traditional IRA   27

Chapter 4—S & P 500   29

How You Can Invest in the S&P 500 With Little Money?   32

Chapter 5—Common Stock   33

How do you define a stock?   36
What do you get by being an owner?   36
How is a stock represented?   36
Why do companies issue stock?   37

The different types of stocks	37
Common stock	38

Chapter 6—Preferred Stock — 39

What is a preferred stock?	41
Features of preferred stocks	41
Different types of preferred stocks	43
What Is The Difference Between Preferred Stock And Common Stock?	46

Chapter 7—The REIT — 49

How Do You Define Real Estate Investment Trust 'REIT'?	51
How you can invest in Real Estate Investment Trust - REIT	52
How to do things the REIT way	53
So what is a REIT company?	53
What are the advantages of buying a REIT?	54
How You Can Pick the Right REIT	55
REITs in the United States	57

Chapter 8—Closed End Funds — 59

What is a Closed-End Fund?	61
What Distinguishes Closed-End Funds from Open-End Funds?	62

Chapter 9—MLPs — 65

How Is a Partnership Classified as an MLP?	68
Have a Look at the MLP Advantage	68
Tax Implications for MLPs	68

Chapter 10—Ex Dividend Date	71
How Do Ex-Dividends Work?	74
What Happens To the Stock's Value?	74
Some More Details	75
Additional Considerations for Mutual Funds	75
Chapter 11—Monthly Dividends and Quarterly Dividends	77
Monthly Dividends	79
Are Monthly Dividends Useful?	79
What Are Monthly Dividend Stocks?	80
How Are Monthly Dividend Stocks Different from Normal Stocks?	80
How Can Monthly Dividend Stocks Help You?	80
How You Can Search for Monthly Dividend Stocks?	81
Can Monthly Dividend Stocks Fit in Your Portfolio?	82
Advantages of Investing in Monthly Dividend Stocks	82
Quarterly Dividends	85
Some Important Dates You Need to Remember	85
Some More Advice on Quarterly Dividends	87
Why Should You Invest in Quarterly Dividend Stocks	87
Chapter 12—Stock Market Sectors	89
Why are Stocks Classified into Different Sectors?	92
Differences between an Industry and a Sector	92
Stock Classification – Things You Need to Keep in Mind	94

Defensive Stocks	94
Cyclical Stocks	95
Defensive or Cyclical – Which Stock is Better?	96
The Concept of Cyclical and Defensive Stocks	97
The Violent Nature of Cyclical Stocks	98
Do Your Research and Get Your Investment Timing Right	99
Investing in the Stock Market – What You Need to Know	101
Quick Recap: Importance of Stock Market Research, Evaluation and Industry Analysis	103

Chapter 13—Risk and Reward — 107

Measuring and Evaluating Risks in Any Investment	110
How You Can Define 'Risk'	110
Different Types of Risks	111
Market Risk	111
Default Risk	112
Interest Rate Risk	113
Liquidity Risk	113
The 'Risk/Reward Ratio'	113
How Much Money Can You Lose?	114
What is Your Comfort Level?	116
How You Can Take Control of Your Risk/Reward Ratio	116

Chapter 14—My Dad's Retirement Plan — 119

Your Game Plan – Setting up Investment Goals	121
Planning Your Investment Amount	122
Choosing Your Investment Strategy	123
Stick to Your Investment Plan	123

Quick Reminder – What is Your Tolerance Level for Investment Risk?	124
The Ten Commandments – My Dad's Retirement Plan	128

Chapter 15—How to Choose a Dividend Stock: Past Performance is Usually a Good Indicator — 139

Fundamental Analysis	143
Qualitative Analysis	143
Value Investing	145
Growth Investing	145
GARP Investing	147
Income Investing	148
CAN SLIM	150
Dogs of the Dow	153
Technical Analysis	154

Chapter 16—Setting up a Dividend Portfolio — 155

How You Can Set Up Your Portfolio	158

Chapter 17—Opening your own Account — 161

Disclaimer

© John Kleemann, 2014. All Rights Reserved.

This Book is intended for people interested in seeking a retirement plan. The author has exercised caution, care and judgment during preparation and research for this Book. However, the author and/or publisher bear(s) no responsibility for any loss that occurs due to a misrepresentation of the information contained within.

The purpose of the Dividends Book is purely informational. It is meant to educate the readers about how stock investments can be used to accumulate wealth over a period of time and ensure financial security after retirement. The information should not be taken as professional investment advice. The resources used for collection of data are reliable to the extent of our knowledge. We bear no responsibility for inaccuracies.

No part of the information presented in the Dividends Book can be reproduced or stored in any form including print or electronic without prior permission from the author. Once you start reading the Dividends Book, it will be acknowledged as you having read the disclaimer.

The stock market is subject to frequent changes and fluctuations because of the high volatility. New trends emerge from time to time. The risk of not benefiting from the investment method covered in this is book is quite possible. You can use the advice and guidance available through the Dividends Book to engage in stock investment but we hold no liability for any losses you incur.

Summary

The Power of Dividend Income Revealed, and How You Can Apply It RIGHT NOW to Your Own Financial Situation!

Are in your 30's, 40's, 50's... or even later? Then here is something you'd be wise to think about...

Are you relying upon Social Security to fund your retirement years? If so, the long and short of it is this:

You're going to find yourself in a world of hurt.

Make No Mistake:

- Your Taxes Will Be Going Higher...

- Benefits & "Loopholes" Will Be Slashed...

- Social Security Will Be Raided Again and Again...

Here's the dirty little open secret about Social Security: There isn't a penny in the so-called trust fund. Every cent that comes into Social Security goes out to pay current government obligations and entitlements. The "trust fund" is replaced with an IOU from Uncle Sam.

Forgive me, but somehow a politician's promise to repay doesn't give me the warm-fuzzies right now.

What Are YOU Doing About YOUR Future Financial Plans?

Let me be blunt, if you are content letting someone else dictate your future and your retirement income, stop reading. This message and this book aren't for you.

The cold, hard truth is this... if you don't **plan and take action now**, you're going to be left holding a very small bag filled with increasingly worthless paper, instead of enjoying a secure flow of income - allowing you to relish the best years of your life.

That's what **the Dividends Book** is all about – making absolutely, dead-on certain you'll be one of those **proactive individuals whose retirement assets will survive – and even thrive** – in the coming tumultuous years ahead.

Pragmatic, Down to Earth, Actionable Information!

The rock-solid information in the Dividends Book won't coddle you with feel-good scenarios or pie-in-the-sky projections that simply won't exist – <u>can't exist</u> – in our present day economy. You'll uncover how things truly are, uncomfortable as that may be.

Make no mistake... The Dividends Book explains in concrete terms what you MUST be doing - right now – to **positively ensure your wealth** not only survives, but thrives in the years ahead.

Three Crucial Factors

When going through the Dividends Book, you're going to uncover three crucial factors about planning for your own retirement…

- **Factor One**: The "Commonly Accepted Wisdom" about your money - which is totally, absolutely WRONG! (What if everything you thought was true… wasn't! Like savings accounts and government bonds are worthwhile investments – FALSE!)

- **Factor Two**: What your bank, your accountant, even your current investment advisors aren't telling you about handling your money & investments. (They either don't know, or they just aren't talking!)

- **Factor Three**: Understanding **the crucial types of investment incomes you must know**, and most importantly how to **identify and capture those investment dollars** so they land in your pocket, and not unnecessarily and unknowingly transferred away to some overpaid advisor or broker. (And yes, I'm not merely talking tens, but more often than not, hundreds of thousands of dollars over the course of your working life!)

Financial Heresy Exposed

Inconceivable, Unimaginable Debt

The "official" U.S. debt was pegged at **16.39 TRILLION DOLLARS**. The ante's just been raised by yet another trillion. The unofficial but truer national debt is actually over four times as great – <u>71 TRILLION</u> DOLLARS.

- $17 trillion or $71 trillion, take your pick. Either way, these numbers are so **insanely, staggering huge**, I doubt anyone can truly grasp their enormity.

- Let's say you were one of the very first "modern men" to do some serious stargazing at the tail end of the **Middle Paleolithic period, and started squandering a <u>MILLION BUCKS</u> a day**. You would still not be approaching the end of your 17 trillion dollar spending orgy, *438 centuries later*. (You'd have to be one of the very first **homo-sapiens** walking the earth to dole out 71 trillion!)

Remember, the government is looking for all the cash it can lay its hands on, but it **only has three ways** of filling its coffers...

- Tax

- Confiscate

- Print & Inflate

We're seeing all three of these going into hyper-drive as I write.

Dividends Book is No-Nonsense Advice, a Field Guide for Financial Success – Let's Take a Peek Inside...

- Do you know the Rule of 72? You should, as it determines how quickly (or not!) your money is going to grow

- How about **DRIPS**? It's one the MOST POWERFUL METHODS for re-investing your money – automatically. Dividends Book shows you how it's done – and done right.

- **ROTH IRA's, Individual IRA's, SEP IRA's** – Do you know the differences between these three popular retirement plans, and the pros & cons of each? You will, after reading this book!

- **Standard & Poor's 500 Index** – What is it, and how will it help you with your retirement planning?

- **Common Stocks vs. Preferred Stocks** – How will your dividend incomes be affected by holding one over another?

- **REITs** – Equity REITs, Mortgage REITs, Hybrid REITs. These are some of the least known and **most overlooked investment** options. Dividends Book spells out exactly what they are, and how to SUCCESSFULLY leverage them in your retirement portfolio.

- **Closed-End vs. Open-End Funds** – What's the difference between them, and which one should you consider when investing your money?

- **MLPs - Master Limited Partnerships**. The simple rule to remember when working with MLPs, why an MLP can be so advantageous, and how the money received from MLPs can mean large tax breaks for you and your retirement!

- **Ex-Dividend Date** (or reinvestment date). How is it determined, and why a single day can make a substantial difference in the dividends you'll receive.

- **Monthly Dividend & Quarterly Dividend Stocks** – How to find them, and how to use these investment opportunities for smoothing out and supporting your monthly income during retirement.

- **Four Key Dividend Dates to Remember**. There are four important dates to consider when dealing with dividends, and yes – The Dividends Book lays out what they are and why you should care.

- **Market Sectors**. Do you know what a "Defensive" stock is? (It has nothing to do with the military!) How about cyclical stocks? What sectors make up each? When is one better than the other? How do you choose between the many and various sectors? The Dividends Book has you covered here as well!

- **Nine Rules For Prosperous Investing.** Follow these rules when investing in the market, and your emotions will take backseat to financial reality – saving you a busload of headaches and a ton of money in the process.

- **Risk, Remorse and Reward.** Yes, all investments have some risk. Keep your money in a bank, and there are still risks – not the least being that your money will actually SHRINK in size over time. (That old dragon named Inflation at work.) We'll discuss the **four actual types of market risk**, and how you can determine which level is best for you and your unique circumstances.

The Dividends Book in Action!

- **Setting Goals** – This will be the backbone of your individual retirement plan. Remember, you can't get to where you want to be if you don't know how to get there!

- How Much to Invest - Setting **SPECIFIC AMOUNTS** is the key!

- **Choosing Your Strategies** – Aggressive, High Risk or Conservative, Low Risk? What suits your style?

- What's Your Risk Level? The **Seven Factors** influencing your overall risk tolerance explained.

- **The Ten Commandments!** Specific, actionable rules to follow for planning your Dividend portfolio – and cashing in when the time is ripe!

- Sticking With It – The **Six Rules of Engagement** to Follow!

- **How to Choose a Dividend Stock.** Actually, you DON'T have to be an investment guru for picking consistent winners. Follow the detailed advice in the Dividends Book, and you'll be nailing down those lucrative dividend payouts time after time.

- The World According to **GARP & CAN SLIM**. Dividends Book takes your investing strategy to the next level by revealing the ins and outs of these two powerful hybrid methods.

- **DOGS of the DOW.** Sounds almost like something out of Shakespeare… (Cry havoc and let slip the Dogs of the Dow!) But contrary to what you may think, these Dogs have a healthy bark when it comes to providing high dividend yields. But be careful, because you have to have your eye on them at all times. We'll show you how to avoid their bite – and keep those dividends flowing.

- Opening Up Your Own Investment Accounts. Sure, you can use a broker – and pay outrageous broker fees. Or you can follow the advice in the Dividends Book, and **take charge of your own affairs**. We'll show you how truly **simple and easy** it is!

Introduction

Introduction

The Rockefeller's, Walton's, DuPont's, and Mellon's all have a closely guarded secret to preserving their fortunes for their families. These families have grown and maintained their wealth, passing it down generation after generation. The closely guarded secret is that these families invest in company stocks that pay consistently increasing dividends. Dividends Book is based on this principle. In this book you will learn, step by step, on how to invest like a dividend millionaire.

If you are young and just starting out, about to retire, or are already retired and want to increase your returns, then this book is for you.

Chapter 1
The Millionaire's Secret

1
The Millionaire's Secret

The Power of Compound Dividends

Albert Einstein was perhaps the biggest proponent of compound interest. He described it both as the 'eighth wonder of the world' and the 'most powerful force in the universe'. For a man of his intelligence and stature to say such a thing about anything adds genuine credibility.

While compound interest is a concept almost exclusive to banks and financial institutions, investors have a new avenue to benefit from compounding: dividends.

In fact, the power of dividend compounding has truly come to the forefront over the years. The basic concept behind compounding is so simple yet highly effective. The idea is that you earn interest on both the principle as well as the interest you have earned previously. Confused? Here is an example to help you out.

The Rolling Snowball

Have you ever seen a snowball rolling down an inclined plane? When it starts off, the snowball is small in size. As it keeps rolling, it starts increasing in size. This is because it collects the snow from the path it rolls down on its way. As its size increases, so does its momentum. It starts descending much faster than it was doing before. The longer the ball keeps rolling, the bigger it will get.

Theoretically, the slope will end causing the snowball to stop. The process of continuum when it comes to compounding interest means that your earnings continue to grow seemingly endlessly. In current economic conditions, people are looking for alternatives to historically low bank interest. You needn't worry as compounding dividends is a perfectly viable vehicle for increasing your return on investment.

Ideal for Long-Term Investors

From the onset, you have to keep one thing in mind: compounding dividends is a long-term strategy. Only investors who are in it for the long haul should consider this option. Remember that you need to let the snowball roll for as long as possible for it to increase in size.

What this means is that investors should look beyond capital gains to benefit from dividend investing. The general perception among investors is to earn dividends on their stock and use them to pay off their bills. In short, the dividends they receive are an income stream which is more often not exhausted before the next payout is made by the company.

In that case, the only way your investment would grow over time is through an increase in the share prices. However, share prices have the tendency to move both upwards and downwards. No one can guarantee that the price of any stock will stay increase or just stay constant. Even the most successful companies see a dip of a few points in their stock prices from time to time.

The Rule of 72

Generally, experienced investors are familiar with the rule of 72. It states that you can divide '72' by the rate of return on an investment and find out the number of years it would take for that investment to double.

Let's say you have an investment earning 6% a year. All you have to do is simply divide 72 by 6 and you get 12. This means that the investment would take 12 years to double. If you had invested $10,000, you will have $20,000 in your pocket after a dozen years have gone by.

Interest compounding has lost its charm simply because banks are paying 1% or less on the money you keep with them. That would mean it would take 72 years for your money to double. This option is only valid for people who are going to live beyond 100.

Coming back to the point, being a shrewd investor requires you to spot opportunities where you can enjoy high returns on investment. That way, you can multiply your investment several times over during the course of two decades or so.

However, applying the Rule of 72 on dividend compounding is tricky. The snowball effect means that the original investment would keep increasing with each passing year. Hence, there isn't a constant number you can use to divide 72 by.

Dividend Growth with Compounding

The rule of compounding requires you to leave the dividends you earn as they are. You don't have the luxury of spending them if you want to compound. The money you earn in the form of dividends is used to buy more stock of the company you have originally invested in.

That way, your original investment increases. Since dividends are paid out per share, the larger number of shares guarantees a higher dividend the next time around for you. Your dividends will keep on accumulating. Not only will your original stock keep earning dividends but also the shares you purchased with the dividends you earned.

Over a period of time, the snowball increases in size. As mentioned above, the bigger it gets, the faster it grows. It is only a matter of time before your stockholding and dividend earnings grow into a substantial amount. With each subsequent period, you will earn more in dividends. In essence, this is double compounding as you are purchasing stocks through two channels.

Believe it or not, businesses actually have infrastructure in place for investors who are interested in compounded dividend growth. It is known as Dividend Reinvestment Plans (DRIPs).

Dividends Book

Dividend Reinvestment Plans (DRIPs)

A word of warning for you before starting off: not every company has DRIPs in place. Though more companies start offering dividend reinvestment plans with each year, the total number is still limited. However, that isn't reason for you to feel discouraged. There are more than 900 companies you can set up a DRIP in. So, what exactly is a DRIP?

The name is self-explanatory. A dividend reinvestment plan gives you the option to reinvest the dividends you are earning into the same company. That way, you don't receive any dividends and they are automatically reinvested on your behalf. It is a long-term investment and you can withdraw it after a period of 20 to 25 years.

DRIPs have been around for a while but not many investors are familiar with the concept. Most of them are interested in using their dividends as income and spending it as soon as they receive it. It takes a lot of patience to resist the temptation of spending the money you earned on your investment. It is something you have to learn to do if you want to compound dividends.

Applying the Rule of 72 on DRIPs

The reason I am saying that you should let your dividends compound over 20 or 25 years is because of the rule of 72. Statistics clearly show that an average DRIP pays out at least 4% or 5% per annum. Divide 72 by 4 and you get 18.

That means you can double your original investment in 18 years.

One thing to take into account is that the dividends you earn along the way are added to the original investment. More shares are bought using the money you earned, so over time your shareholding increases considerably. Suppose you buy 100 shares of a company for $10/share for an initial investment of $1000. Let's say the company pays a 5% dividend (annually) to its shareholders. If you reinvest all of your dividends to purchase more shares you will have $2400 at the end of 18 years.

You can see in this example that the power of compounding dividends enables you to double your investment well before the period of 18 years. If we apply the Rule of 72, we see that the money would actually double around the 15th year, but that is not even factoring in that the price of the original investment would likely increase as well. As you can see, with compounding, the number of shares you own after 18 years will have grown substantially.

It doesn't take a rocket scientist to see that the dividends you earn as your number of shares increase would be much more than the initial 100 shares, in fact you would own 229 shares in the company you invested in some 18 years earlier. DRIPs are the perfect channel for you to compound your dividends. Factoring in an increase in share price and an increase in dividend interest it is very possible to double your investment within a decade or so. Stocks with a higher dividend yield can help you achieve that even sooner!

Chapter 2
The DRIP

2
The DRIP

Investing in DRIPs or Dividend Reinvestment Plans has slowly become one of the most popular ways for individuals to invest in the stock market. You will come across a number of companies that allow current shareholders to purchase stocks directly from the company, most importantly by passing the brokers and other brokerage commissions.

If you wonder which type of investors should include DRIPs in their portfolio, this option is viable for investors who are looking for a long term investment and want to buy more ownership with the passage of time.

DRIP investing without a doubt is the best way to go if you want to reinvest your dividends automatically. Once you enroll in a dividend reinvestment plan, you will no longer have to monitor your dividends.

Before moving ahead, let's have a look at some of the perks of dividend reinvestment plans. As mentioned earlier, DRIPs are an ideal way for you (the shareholder) to reinvest variable amounts of money in a company. As a result of reinvesting, you can purchase shares of some of the well-known companies, less the usual commission.

Instead of giving you the quarterly investment check, the company, brokerage firm or transfer agent running the dividend reinvesting plan uses the money to buy additional shares of the company in your name.

If you are a shareholder of the company that operates the DRIP itself, you will be notified about the specific times in the year when you are allowed to purchase shares under the DRIP program.

Dividend Reinvestment Plan (DRIP) – Investor's Benefits

1. Company operated dividend reinvesting plans are commission free. Since there is no broker to facilitate the process, this reinvestment plan is very attractive to small investors. You don't have to save up a lot of funds for a long period of time to pay the traditional brokerage commission.

2. Some companies running DRIP's allow you to purchase additional shares using cash directly from the company. This cash purchase is normally offered at a 1 – 10 % discount and there is no extra fee attached. Since there is no additional fee attached, the cost of these shares as an investor is considerably lower than what you have to pay if you purchased the shares outside of a dividend reinvestment plan.

3. The best part about dividend reinvestment plan is that it is flexible. You can invest large and small amounts depending on what suits you at that point in time. Most DRIP's allow you to invest amount as large as $500,000 or as small as $10 at one time. You are less likely to find a plan that allows reinvestment lower than $10.

4. Dividend reinvestment plans involve a technique called **Dollar Cost Averaging.** The price at which you buy stocks is averaged out using this system and you would never end up buying stocks when the prices are high up or really low

You may be wondering why companies initiate dividend reinvestment plans and encourage shareholders to join the program. Companies get low cost access to capital and develop a stable shareholder base. Due to the increasing popularity of DRIPs, more and more companies are setting up this plan.

DRIP – Joining the Plan

Joining a dividend reinvestment plan is easy and here's how you can do it.

Don't jump into the first offer you find, instead focus on companies that give you the best long term investment. Just because a company offers a DRIP does not mean it is a good investment option.

Remember, investing in a dividend reinvestment plan initiated by a bad company will never give you a good return. You need to focus on your investment on companies that have strong financials and give you favorable growth opportunities.

Once you have decided to become part of a dividend reinvestment plan, you can contact the company's shareholder service department to check whether they have a plan.

Dividends Book

Another thing you need to keep in mind is that dividend reinvestment plan specifics and eligibility can vary from one company to another. Some companies may allow you to join the plan even when you own only one share, while others require you to own at least 50 shares before you can become eligible.

While dividend reinvestment plans offer optional cash purchases, the timing and frequency of these purchases can vary greatly between plans. Remember, it is very important that you talk to the company's shareholder service department before joining a DRIP. You need to do your homework before hand especially if you don't want to find out afterwards that you need more shares to enroll in the company's DRIP.

In order to enroll in most dividend reinvestment plans, you must own at least one share of stock of the company and it is has to be registered in your name, not the street or brokerage name. The number of shares you need to own can vary from one company to another, but they all need to be registered in your own name.

Once you find out all the details and select a stock investment, you have to find out whether your desired firm is offering a dividend reinvestment plan. Request your company to send you a DRIP enrollment form, and a prospectus. If you use an online brokerage firm there will be a form online.

Fill out your form correctly and clearly specify whether you want all or some of your dividend reinvested. Some companies also allow you to reinvest dividends partially and more information on this is available from company sources.

Once you are done, return the completed form to the company and begin investing via the dividend reinvestment plan. If you are anxious to start investing via optional cash payment, make sure you read the rules put down by the company.

Most companies do their best to help you keep track of your reinvestment and you will receive statements after every successful reinvestment. It is important that you maintain a record of these statements as they are required when you want to resell shares.

Why DRIP?

If you are looking for options to build wealth over a long haul, it is not easy to find an option that is as good as dividend reinvestment plans. As mentioned earlier, instead of buying shares from the stock market, you purchase the shares directly from the company on a regular basis. Dividends you earn automatically go into purchasing more shares from the company and in many cases you can purchase additional shares using the company's cash purchase option.

If you are still not sure why you should invest your money in a dividend reinvestment plan, here is a brief overview to help you get a better idea.

DRIPs are very popular for the reason that you can start your investment with very little capital. Moreover, you can purchase stocks and build wealth by paying a very low or

Dividends Book

no fee. This is a distinct advantage if you want to start your investment on a planned budget.

At the start of the process, you can own the stocks of just one company, and as you get familiar with the way dividend reinvestment plans work, you can diversify your portfolio and become part of a number of different DRIPs.

Dividend reinvestment plans offer a number of advantages other than starting off with a minimum amount of capital. You can actually invest at your own pace and generally you can make your plans based on your personal preferences. Since your dividends are reinvested on a regular schedule, you can buy more shares without paying any extra commission.

One great advantage to DRIPs is that you save money on broker commissions. Since there is no "middleman" or broker involved in the process, you can actually save money in transaction costs. You don't have to pay a fee every time you make an investment or hire professional services. When less money goes out of your pocket as broker commissions, more money will be left with you to make further investments.

Another reason new investors prefer dividend reinvestment plans is because there are less chances of getting emotional. Of course every investor will be tempted to buy shares when the market is doing well, but this scenario can be changed very soon as fear of economic downturn forces them to "sell" the shares.

If you enroll in a dividend reinvestment plan, you commit yourself to investing on a regular schedule and the market condition has minimal effect on the way you invest. No matter if times are good or bad, you can acquire more shares slowly and your wealth will surely continue to build.

DRIPs should be your choice if you cannot resist the temptation to cash out your dividends and spend your money. When you are part of a dividend reinvestment plan, every single penny you earn is automatically reinvested to purchase additional shares of the company. This means you don't receive a dividend check so there is no point in talking about how you should control your spending.

Enrolling in a dividend reinvestment plan is also a good decision if you don't want the current market conditions to influence your investment. As mentioned earlier, DRIPs implement the Dollar Cost Averaging strategy and reinvest your dividends according to a schedule. And, all this happens regardless of the current market scenario or current share price of your stock.

Chapter 3
Roth IRA versus Traditional IRA

3
Roth IRA versus Traditional IRA

An Individual Retirement Arrangement or IRA is a form of retirement plan that is offered by a number of financial institutions. These retirement plans offer tax advantages for retirement savings in the U.S. You will come across several different types of IRAs including:

Traditional IRA

This type of IRA is held at an institution such as a bank or brokerage. You can invest anything that the institution allows including certificates of deposit, stocks and mutual funds. Contributions made to a Traditional IRA are often tax deductible.

Roth IRA

A Roth IRA or Individual Retirement Arrangement is a special type of retirement plan under U.S. laws. If you compare Roth IRAs with other retirement plans, the most obvious difference you will see is that a Roth IRA grants a tax break on the money that is withdrawn from the original plan during retirement. In simple words, withdrawals from Roth IRA are usually tax free.

SEP IRA

Simplified Employee Pension Individual Retirement Arrangement or SEP IRA is a great choice for small business owners to provide retirement plans for the business owners and their employees. Funds in Simplified Employee Pension Individual Retirement Arrangements can be invested the same way as other IRAs.

Other types of IRAs include Simple IRAs and Self Directed IRAs.

Roth IRA – The Larger Picture

Roth IRA is one option you can consider to enjoy your golden years of retirement. There are many ways you can save money over the years and turn extra cash into savings, but the question is "what if you don't have extra cash?" Luckily, Roth IRAs allow you to "invest" money and earn a sizable profit.

As mentioned earlier the Roth IRA or Roth Individual Retirement Arrangement is a special type of retirement plan that allows you to withdraw money from the plan without being taxed, provided certain conditions are met.

How is Roth IRA Different?

The working of Roth IRA is different when compared to other types of IRAs including Traditional IRAs. If you want to know more about the most obvious advantages of a Roth IRA, here is a brief summary.

Dividends Book

1. Direct contributions you make to a Roth IRA may be withdrawn any time and this withdrawal is tax free. Traditional IRAs work differently as your withdrawals are taxed as ordinary income.

2. Converted contributions held in a Roth IRA maybe withdrawn tax free after the seasoning period (which currently is 5 years).

3. Distributions from a Roth IRA do not count towards your Adjusted Gross Income. This means distributions from a Roth IRA do not increase your marginal income tax bracket or cause other income to be taxed higher.

4. If your Roth IRA account has money due to a conversion from a Traditional IRA, you can withdraw the total converted amount without paying a penalty as long as you have passed the seasoning period (which currently is five years).

5. You can make contributions to a Roth IRA even if you are participating in other qualified retirement plans such as a 401(k).

6. In the case when a Roth IRA owner dies, the owner's beneficiary becomes the sole owner. Even if the beneficiary owns a separate Roth IRA, she/he can combine both the Roth IRAs into one plan without paying a penalty.

7. Assets in the Roth IRA can be passed on to heirs.

Roth IRA Investment Options

Named after the late Senator William V. Roth Jr. a Roth Individual Retirement Arrangement helps people save for retirement. You are free to invest money into a Roth IRA and some of the options you can choose include common stocks, bonds and mutual funds. Other options are certificates of deposit (CDs), derivatives, notes and real estate.

Calculating Roth IRA Gains

You will be surprised to know that younger people can make the most of their money by investing in a Roth Individual Retirement Arrangement. As a 25 year old, you can contribute a maximum of $5,500* to Roth IRA annually (* based on 2013 value).

Let's assume you invest $5,500 one time and get 8.0% gain annually on the money. After five years, your total amount would be approx. $7,700 and after 10 years, your $5500 investment would be over $10,000.

Isn't this great? Just imagine the amount your initial investment will make when you reach the retirement age. This does not mean that senior citizens cannot contribute to a Roth IRA. In fact you can contribute $6,500* annually if you are at least 50 years old (based on 2013 value). Even if you contribute $6,500 once, the amount will be more than $12,000 at an 8.0% return rate over the period of ten years.

Simply put, your one time investment doubles and you can make substantially more money if you contribute $6,500 annually, every year after you reach 50 years.

Eligibility for Roth IRA

A Roth IRA has eligibility criteria and income limitations. Congress has set limits for every person who can contribute to a Roth IRA based upon income.

As a taxpayer, you can contribute $5,500 (age 49 and below) or $6,500 (age 50 or above) to Roth IRA only if you your annual income is below the maximum Modified Adjusted Gross Income level that is set.

If your filing status is...	And your modified AGI is...	Then you can contribute...
married filing jointly or qualifying widow(er)	< $178,000	up to the limit
	≥ $178,000 but < $188,000	a reduced amount
	≥ $188,000	Zero
married filing separately and you lived with your spouse at any time during the year	< $10,000	a reduced amount
	≥ $10,000	Zero
single, head of household, or married filing separately and you did not live with your spouse at any time during the year	< $112,000	up to the limit
	≥ $112,000 but < $127,000	a reduced amount
	≥ $127,000	Zero

[1]

---

[1] Source: http://www.irs.gov/Retirement-Plans/Amount-of-Roth-IRA-Contributions-That-You-Can-Make-For-2013

For more information regarding Roth IRA contributions, visit http://www.irs.gov/Retirement-Plans/Amount-of-Roth-IRA-Contributions-That-You-Can-Make-For-2013.

Traditional IRA – The Larger Picture

Choosing the best retirement plan does become a confusing task when you have so many options. It is not easy to figure out a plan that is best for your situation. This section looks at the Traditional Individual Retirement Accounts or Traditional IRA to help you decide whether or not this is the right plan for you.

The Traditional IRA is also an excellent way to boost your retirement income. You can make contributions at your own discretion, so this plan is really convenient. Perhaps the biggest advantage of a Traditional IRA is that you have the option to convert it to Roth IRA. A Roth IRA on the other hand cannot be converted into a Traditional IRA.

A Major Disadvantage of Traditional IRA

One thing to keep in mind is that withdrawals in Traditional IRAs must begin when you reach 70½ years, more precisely, by April 1 of the calendar year after you reach 70½ years.

If you fail to make the required withdrawal, half of the mandatory amount you were supposed to withdraw will be owed to the IRS in the form of penalties. The Roth IRA is completely free of these requirements.

Places to Establish Traditional IRA

A Traditional IRA can only be established at a place that has IRS approval to offer IRAs. Examples include banks and brokerage companies.

Roth vs. Traditional IRA

Now that you know about both the Roth and Traditional IRA, it is time to figure out which plan is better. As a tax payer you may wonder which type of IRA – Roth or Traditional is a good choice in your case.

With The Traditional IRA you receive the tax deduction at the time of contribution. The Traditional IRA cannot be withdrawn without penalty until you are 59 ½.

When you do start withdrawing your money at 59 ½, you are required to pay the normal tax rate on the money based on your income.

With the Roth IRA you can contribute as you go along, but you do not receive a tax deduction. But the biggest advantage is all proceeds including your gains are tax free at the time of withdrawal.

Let us see how powerful this is. If you invest at age 29, $5,000 per year in a Roth IRA until you are age 65, and assuming it averages 9 percent per year, your investment will be worth $1,286,880.

Yes, you will be a millionaire, and your withdrawals will be tax free. The best part is you will have made 25 percent per year just by being tax free, assuming you are in the average middle income tax bracket, plus your 9 percent. Yes this is completely legal, and approved by our government.

You can see why the Roth IRA is the best retirement plan for most people. Always consult your tax professional to be sure it is the best for you.

Chapter 4
S & P 500

4
S & P 500

The **S&P 500** also known as **Standard & Poor's 500** is a stock market index. It is based on the market capitalizations of companies traded on the U.S. stock market and includes 500 leading companies, with some located outside the U.S.

The reason Standard & Poor's 500 is different from popular indices in U.S. stock markets such as the Dow Jones Industrial Average and the Nasdaq is the fact that it is far more diverse and has a better weighting methodology. Most experts believe that it is the best representation of the U.S. stock market and the U.S. economy as well.

The **S&P 500** index is maintained by Standard & Poor's which is a division of McGraw-Hill. McGraw-Hill on the other hand is known to publish other popular stock market indices including S&P Composite 1500, S&P MidCap 400 and S&P SmallCap 600.

Even Fortune 500 tries to list the 500 largest companies by gross revenue but the list is generated regardless of whether or not company stocks are traded publicly. The Fortune 500 index also ignores companies that are located outside the United States.

How You Can Invest in the S&P 500 With Little Money?

One of the biggest challenges for any investor is to decide how big or how small their investment can be. Just a few decades back, most brokerages and mutual funds required that investors bring in a decent amount of money to the table to get started. Minimum deposits of $1,000 or $500 were pretty common even after leading discounts.

If you want to invest in the S&P 500, it is important that you find a brokerage that allows you to invest with a very low trading fee. You then have several possibilities. One of the best things to do would be to open an account with a discount brokerage and then buy an S&P 500 exchange-traded fund.

Low cost brokerages such as Scottrade.com and Etrade.com allow you to open accounts with low minimum deposits and you can then buy one share of an S&P 500 exchange-traded fund for the current market price. This way you can own the S&P 500 for less than $70, however you'll need to pay the commission each time you invest in the S&P 500 or when you sell your share.

The bottom line is that you can become part of the S&P 500 even if you have less than $200 to invest.

Chapter 5
Common Stock

5
Common Stock

You would love to see money rolling in without having to show up at a company after you retire. This situation sounds a little strange, but it is a lot closer to reality – a lot closer than what you think.

Most of you would have probably guessed it by now. We have discussed a variety of investment options and it is now time to talk about owning stocks. Well, stocks are a fabulous tool that you can use to build your wealth. This is one of the prime reasons stocks are part of nearly every "ideal" investment portfolio.

Before you start investing in stocks and start your road to financial freedom, it is important that you have a basic understanding of stocks and how they work.

If you have a good look around, you'll see that every other person is interested in the stock market. What was once limited only to the "rich", is now being used even by a common man for growing wealth. The increasing interest in the stock market has encouraged every one to become a stock owner.

How do you define a stock?

In simple words, stock is a share in the ownership of a company. When you own a company's stock, you can actually claim the company's assets and earnings. As you own more stocks in the company, you gain more ownership. So whether you own shares, stock or equity, it all means the same thing.

What do you get by being an owner?

When you buy a company's stock, you join the other owners (shareholders) of the company and all of you have the right to claim everything the company owns. This means you get the share in every trademark and contract of the company. Moreover, you have a share in the company's earnings as well as any voting rights that are attached to the stock.

How is a stock represented?

In the past, stocks were represented by a stock certificate. You would get a fancy piece of paper to prove your ownership, but now your brokerage features an electronic copy of the records. You had to take the physical document along with you whenever you wanted to sell your shares. Now, things have changed a great deal and you can actually sell your shares with a simple mouse click or a phone call.

After reading through the discussion on the previous pages, you know that being a shareholder gives you the right to claim a share in a company's assets and profits. Profits can also be paid in the form of dividends and you can refer to the section on Dividend Reinvestment Plans (DRIPs) to learn more. DRIPs are a great way to purchase stocks directly from a reputable company and invest small amounts of money at regular intervals.

Another important thing you need to keep in mind is that being a stock owner does not make you liable if the company is unable to pay its debts. If you own a particular company's stock and the company goes bankrupt, the maximum value you will lose is the total value of your investment. Your personal assets remain unharmed so you can say that stocks have limited liability. This surely is a beneficial feature as you would never lose "everything" you own!

Why do companies issue stock?

Some of you might ask why companies issue stocks when they could keep the profit for themselves. Well, companies share their profit because at some point or other, every organization needs to raise money. This means companies need to borrow money from another party or raise money by selling a small part of their company. The latter is what is known as issuing stocks.

The different types of stocks

Common stocks and preferred stocks are the two most common types of stocks. It is possible that companies come up with different ideas and customize different types of stocks in any way they prefer.

Dividends Book

Common stock

Common stock, as the name suggests is quite common. In fact, the majority of the stocks issued by companies are in this form and when people discuss stocks, they are most likely referring to common stocks.

If you talk about the features of common stocks, you will see that common stocks give you an ownership share in the company and you can also claim your right (dividends) on a defined portion of the profits.

Common stocks yield higher returns than any other form of investment when held for a long period of time. This however, makes them a more risky investment. Remember, if common stocks give you a higher return, they also have greater risks. This is because if your company goes bankrupt and liquidates, you (the common shareholder) will not receive any money until all other creditors, preferred shareholders and bond holders receive their payment.

Other terms such as voting share or ordinary share are also used to describe common stocks in other parts of the world whereas common stocks is mainly used in the United States.

Chapter 6
Preferred Stock

6
Preferred Stock

What is a preferred stock?

Preferred stocks also give you some ownership rights in a company, but you don't get the same voting rights. If you become a preferred stockholder, you can guarantee a fixed dividend. This feature is quite different from common stocks where dividends are never fixed or guaranteed.

Another distinct advantage of owning preferred stocks is that you are paid off before other common shareholders, i.e. right after debt holders. On the other hand, preferred stocks are callable, meaning the company can purchase the preferred stocks from the shareholders at anytime.

Features of preferred stocks

Preferred stocks have a number of interesting features and preferences including:

1. Preference in dividends*

2. Preference in assets especially in case of liquidation

3. Conversion to common stock

4. Non-voting

5. Callable – the corporation or company can call the shares anytime

   * Preference here does not mean guaranteed dividend payments, however you will be preferred over a common stock owner when the company is paying the stated dividend rate.

   Another thing you need to consider is that preferred stocks can be **cumulative or noncumulative**.

   Cumulative preferred stocks mean that if you fail to receive a dividend, the company needs to make up for it later. Your dividends will accumulate with every dividend period that passes i.e. quarterly, semi-annually or annually. All missed dividends on cumulative preferred stock become part of the dividend arrears.

   Non cumulative or straight preferred stocks are without this feature. This means if you don't get the dividends on time, all passed dividends would be lost.

   Some other features of preferred stocks include:

1. Preferred stock may or may not have fixed liquidation value associated with it.

2. Preferred stock owners can claim on liquidation proceeds of a stock corporation. This claim can be equal to the liquidation value unless otherwise stated or negotiated.

3. Majority of preferred stocks have a fixed dividend amount, which is usually mentioned as a percentage of par value.

4. If a preferred stock dividend is not fixed, then it can be floating, i.e. change according to a standard interest-rate index.

5. Some preferred stocks also have special voting rights in special events. These include voting rights when new shares are issued or when new directors are elected. Preferred stocks otherwise have no voting rights associated with them.

6. Preferred stocks can also gain voting rights in some cases especially when dividends are in arrears for a considerable period of time.

7. Preferred stocks in the United States usually have a call provision. This means the issuing company can repurchase its shares at its own discretion.

Different types of preferred stocks

Even preferred stocks are quite diverse in nature. In addition to straight preferred stocks, you will come across many different types of preferred stocks including:

1. **Prior Preferred Stock**

These have the highest priority when compared to other preferred stocks. If the company only has money to pay dividends on any one of the preferred stocks, it will pay the prior preferred stockholders. This means prior preferred stocks have less credit risk than other forms of preferred stocks.

2. Preference Preferred Stock

Preference preferred stocks are also highly ranked and they come right after the company's prior preferred stocks. You would be preferred over all other types of company's preferred stocks, except for prior preferred stocks.

If the company issues more than one preference preferred stock, they will be ranked in the order of seniority. For example, stocks issued first will get first preference; those issued second will get second preference, and so on.

3. Convertible Preferred Stock

These are special type of preferred stocks which can be exchanged for a fixed number of company's common stocks. You can decide the time you want to exchange your convertible preferred stock regardless of the market price of the company's common stocks. However, you have to keep one thing in mind. This conversion is non reversible, i.e. you cannot convert your common stocks back to convertible preferred stocks.

4. Cumulative Preferred Stock

As mentioned earlier, if you don't get the dividends on cumulative preferred stock, it will accumulate for the payment that needs to be made in the future.

5. Exchangeable Preferred Stock

As the name suggests, this type of preferred stock can be exchanged for some other security.

6. Participating Preferred Stock

You can get extra dividends when you own participating preferred stocks, only if your company achieves financial goals that are predetermined. Your regular share of dividends would be given regardless of the way your company performs (in case the company performs well enough to settle its due dividend payments.)

Participating preferred stocks allow you to earn extra or additional dividends when the company achieves the predetermined sales or profit goals.

7. Perpetual Preferred Stock

This particular type of preferred stock has no fixed date on which you (the shareholder) will receive the returned invested capital.

8. Putable Preferred Stock

If you own putable preferred stocks, you (the shareholder) can force the issuer (only under certain conditions) to redeem shares.

9. **Monthly Income Preferred Stock**

These stocks basically are a combination of preferred stocks and subordinated debt.

10. **Non-Cumulative Preferred Stocks**

If you don't get the dividends for this type of preferred stock, they will not accumulate to be paid later. This is a common scenario in bank preferred stocks.

What Is The Difference Between Preferred Stock And Common Stock?

Preferred and common stocks differ in two main ways.

First, preferred stockholders have a greater claim to a company's assets and profits when compared to common stockholders. This surely is beneficial if a company has excess profits (cash) and decides to pay dividends to all its investors. If this is the case, preferred stockholders must be paid before common stockholders.

This feature becomes more important when a company can no longer meet its financial obligations and its assets need to be liquidated to clear outstanding debts. This situation is also known as insolvency and here, all common stockholders are the last in line to get paid. In simple words, common stockholders do not receive any payment unless all preferred shareholders are paid out.

Second major difference between the two is that preferred stock dividends are different and generally greater than those of common stock. So if you become a preferred stockholder, you will have a clear idea of when you will be paid. Preferred stock dividends are paid at regular intervals and this is not the case for common stocks on most occasions.

In the case of common stocks, the company's board of directors will decide whether or not they should pay out the dividends to common stockholders. Most people regard preferred stocks as fixed-income security because their dividends or returns do not fluctuate time and again as common stock dividends do.

Adding to this feature is the fact that dividends on preferred stocks are guaranteed. That is, if a company misses out on one payment, it needs to settle it before any future dividends are paid.

Chapter 7
The REIT

7
The REIT

How Do You Define Real Estate Investment Trust 'REIT'?

A REIT is a security that sells like a stock on the major exchanges. You can invest in real estate directly or through real estate properties and mortgages. What makes Real Estate Investment Trusts so popular is the fact that they offer special tax considerations. Moreover, you can also get high yields as an investor. Remember, REITs are a highly liquid method of investing in real estate.

Here are a few terms you will come across when dealing with REITs.

1. Equity REITs

Equity REIT means you invest in and own a real estate property. You will only be responsible for the equity or value of your own real estate assets. Revenue in Real Estate Investment Trusts comes from property rents.

2. Mortgage REITs

As the name suggests, mortgage REITs deal mainly in investment and ownership of real estate property mortgages. These REITs lend money for mortgages and this loan is given to owners of real estate. The loan can be used to purchase existing mortgages or mortgage-backed securities.

Mortgage Real Estate Investment Trusts mainly generate revenue by the interest earned on the mortgage loans.

3. Hybrid REITs

This form of Real Estate Investment Trust combines the investment strategies of equity REITs and mortgage REITs. Hybrid REITs allow you to invest in both properties and mortgages.

How you can invest in Real Estate Investment Trust - REIT

You can invest in REITs either by purchasing shares from an open exchange directly or put your investment in a mutual fund that specializes in public real estate. Here is some more good news for you. You should think about investing in REITs because many of them are accompanied by other favorable investment options such as dividend reinvestment plans (DRIPs).

Among other things, Real Estate Investment Trusts invest in shopping malls, apartments, office buildings, hotels and warehouses. You can find REITs which invest only in one particular area of real estate – office buildings for example.

Some REITs only invest in one specific geographical region i.e. state or country. Remember, investing in real estate investment trusts is a dividend paying means of taking part in the real estate market.

How to do things the REIT way

There are plenty of investment options out there and this creates a challenge for most investors.

Things get really interesting when you get a lot of advice from your friends. For most people, stocks are the core of successful investing. For some, bonds are the safest place to put money and others prefer to put their money in mutual funds.

Real Estate Investment Trusts are not as well-known as these categories and often, they are the most overlooked investment option.

So what is a REIT company?

REIT Company accumulates a pool of money through IPO or Initial Public Offering. This IPO is then used to buy, manage, develop and sell real estate assets. If you compare IPO with other security offerings, it is identical in terms of reporting requirements and regulation.

The difference however, is that instead of purchasing stocks from a single company, the REIT owner is buying a portion of the real estate pool. Yes, you can buy a portion of a managed pool of real estate even if you own one REIT unit. This pool will then generate income through leasing, renting and selling of property, which is distributed to you directly (i.e. the REIT owner) on a regular basis.

What are the advantages of buying a REIT?

Once you buy a share of REIT, you own a physical asset that has a long expected life span and there is a lot of potential to generate income through renting and property appreciation. Not only will you have the ownership rights of a property, you can also participate in the income generated by the property. This creates a sense of security for the investors as you will have a right over your property as well as enjoy the benefits of your income.

Another distinct advantage of buying a REIT is that you can invest without having to put in large amounts of capital or labor. Moreover, as more and more funds are put together in your real estate pool, you can create a greater amount of diversification in your portfolio and buy numerous properties. This is a great way to reduce the problems associated with buying a single asset.

You can imagine it might not be very easy to buy and maintain a large number of investment properties on your own. You would have to put in a substantial amount of time and money in an investment which is not easily liquidated.

On the other hand, if you buy a Real Estate Investment Trust, your capital investment is limited to the price of your unit. The amount of labor you have to put in is equal to the amount of research that is required and lastly, your shares are liquid on regular stock exchanges.

Another thing you need to know is that REITs must distribute nearly 90% of their yearly taxable income, i.e. income produced by real estate to their shareholders. The final and perhaps the most important advantage of buying a REIT is that you will earn a lot of profit as the holder of a REIT.

Also, higher rate of distribution means that you have more chances of making excess cash on your investment. This feature distinguishes REITs from other investments such as common stocks where the company's board of directors decides whether or not extra cash should be distributed to the common stockholder.

How You Can Pick the Right REIT

Like other types of investments, you need to do your homework before deciding which REIT is right for you. Here are some simple tips that will help you with your decision.

1. Understand the track record of the managers and their team.

Before you jump into buying the first portion of managed real estate pool you come across, take some time to understand and evaluate the track record of a company's manager and team.

Remember, profits you earn after buying a REIT are closely related to the manager's ability to identify and pick the right investments. The manager also needs to decide upon the best strategy when choosing the best investment.

2. Have a close look at the diversification of your portfolio.

As mentioned earlier, Real Estate Investment Trusts are more focused on the ownership of property and the real estate market is influenced by location and type of property.

If you decide to buy a REIT, it is crucial that you buy a share only when your desired portfolio is diversified. If your Real Estate Investment Trust is dominated by commercial real estate, you might face problems in the future if there is a drop in occupancy rates.

Your REIT also needs to have sufficient capital to fund future growth initiatives and maintain a diversified portfolio for increased returns.

3. The numbers count!

One final thing that you should keep in mind before buying a specific REIT is its earnings, i.e. funds created from operations and, of course cash that is available for distribution.

Remember, these numbers are very important as they measure the overall performance of the Real Estate Investment Trust and determine the money that will be distributed to you as an investor.

Be careful to not focus only on the numbers generated by the REIT. Remember, the final numbers are only useful if you've looked closely at the other two signs, diversification and the role of management. This is because the money you make is influenced by the diversification of your portfolio as well as the management's choice in picking real estate investments.

The bottom line is that there are a lot of different ways to invest money and increase wealth and this applies to stocks, REITs, bonds, mutual funds, DRIPs and any other investment. With all important decisions, it is crucial that you think clearly and then make a well informed decision. Having said this, REITs also have a great deal of interesting features that make them a good fit in your investment portfolio.

REITs in the United States

REITs are companies that own and operate "income producing" real estate. You will also come across some Real Estate Investment Trusts that actually finance real estate. To qualify as a REIT in the United States, a company must distribute at least 90% of its taxable income to its shareholders in the form of dividends annually. Moreover, under U.S. tax rules, a REIT company must:

1. Have a corporation, trust, or association structure

2. Have a board of directors or trustees to manage the company

3. Have more than 75% of total assets invested in real estate

4. Have valid transferable shares or transferable certificates of interest

5. Have 100 persons or more as joint owners

6. Not be a financial institution or an insurance company

Dividends Book

7. Distribute 90% of its taxable income to its shareholders

8. Have 95% of its income as a result of interest and property income. Moreover, 75% of the company's gross income should come from rents or mortgage interest.

Chapter 8
Closed End Funds

8
Closed End Funds

What is a Closed-End Fund?

A closed-end fund is a publicly traded investment company. It raises funds through Initial Public Offerings (IPOs), which are then listed and traded like a regular stock on a stock exchange. A closed-end fund is also known as "closed-end investment" or "closed-end mutual fund."

Before moving forward, there is something you need to understand. Despite sounding like mutual funds, close-end funds do not have any similarities with the former. Technically, mutual funds are known as open-end funds.

Closed-end funds raise a fixed amount of capital through IPOs by issuing a fixed number of shares, which are then purchased by investors as stock.

On the other hand, open end funds are bought and sold directly from the mutual fund company. In addition, there is no fixed number of shares and a company can continue to create more shares to meet the demand by investors. On the flip side, the investment portfolio can be affected adversely if a large number of shares are redeemed quickly and the company needs to make trades to fulfill the demands of cash created by share redemption.

In a closed-end fund, an investment advisor or fund manager takes care of the IPO proceeds and then invests the shares according to the fund's mandate. Stock prices in the case of closed-end funds can fluctuate according to the changes in market forces (i.e. demand and supply). The prices are also influenced by the changing values of securities held by the fund.

What Distinguishes Closed-End Funds from Open-End Funds?

Some characteristics that distinguish closed-end funds from open-end funds are:

1. Closed-end funds are not open to new capital once they start operating.

2. Shares of closed-end funds are traded on stock exchanges rather than being cashed in directly by the fund.

3. You can trade closed-end fund shares at anytime during the day when the stock market is open. On the other hand, open-end fund shares can only be traded at the time specified by the fund manager. Moreover, the dealing price of shares is not known in advance in the case of open-end shares.

4. Closed-end funds are traded at a premium or discount to its original Net Asset Value. Open-end funds are usually traded at their original Net Asset Value (Changes and adjustments can be made to the Net Asset Value of open-end funds.)

Another feature that distinguishes closed-end funds is the use of leverage to increase yields or returns. Closed-end funds might raise investment capital by issuing preferred stock, long-term debt, auction rate securities or reverse-repurchase agreements. All this is done to earn higher returns on the additional capital that is invested.

Usually closed-end funds use a combination of leveraging techniques; however, they can also use individual tactics. You may come across some closed-end funds that use only one leveraging technique.

If a closed-end fund decides to issue preferred stock, it will create two different types of shareholders, namely preferred stockholders and common stockholders.

Shareholders of preferred stock earn more benefits based on the total managed assets of the fund. Common shareholders on the other hand get distributions based only on the common assets of the fund. This reduces their returns more significantly when compared to the preferred shareholders because common shareholders get returns on a smaller asset base.

Since closed-end fund shares are traded like any other stock, you (the investor) need to pay a brokerage commission. This is not the case in open-ended mutual funds where the brokerage commission varies depending on the class of share that is chosen as well as the method of purchasing the fund.

In simple words, you can say that closed-end funds do not have "sales-based" shares, i.e. shares that differ

Dividends Book

according to commission rates and annual fees. However, loan-participation closed-end funds are an exception.

Closed-end funds can be a great addition to your portfolio. As always, do the research to find a fund that suits your needs.

Chapter 9
MLPs

9
MLPs

Master Limited Partnership (MLP) is a type of limited partnership that is publicly traded. You can observe two different types of partners in this particular partnership. The limited partner in a MLP is the person or group that provides capital and receives income distributions at regular periods from the MLP's cash flow.

The other partner, also known as general partner is the group or party responsible for managing MLP affairs and receives compensation linked to the performance of the venture.

Remember this simple rule: MLPs contain two business entities – limited partner (LP) and general partner (GP). The limited partner invests capital into the partnership venture and receives cash distributions periodically. The general partner (GP) has a close watch over the venture's operations. In addition, the general partner also receives "Incentive Distribution Rights" or IDR.

IDRs provide the general partners with performance based pay, where performance is measured by cash distributions made to the limited partner. Usually, GPs receive 2% of the total LP distribution, but as payment to unit holders increases, the percentage share of general partners through IDRs also increases.

How Is a Partnership Classified as an MLP?

For a partnership to be legally known as an MLP, it needs to derive most (i.e. more than 90%) of its cash flow from real estate, natural resources and commodities. This is the main criteria determining whether or not a partnership can be classified as a Master Limited Partnership.

Have a Look at the MLP Advantage

Perhaps the biggest advantage of an MLP is that it gives you the best combined benefits of a limited partnership with the liquidity of a publicly traded company. The Master Limited Partnership or MLP does not pay taxes directly from the profit and the money is only taxed when unit holders receive their distributions.

Tax Implications for MLPs

Like other limited partnerships, MLPs do not have tax at the company level. This is beneficial in lowering the MLP's cost of capital. There are fewer problems related to double taxation on dividends and companies that become a Master Limited Partnership have a cost advantage over their counterparts that are incorporated.

If you are part of a Master Limited Partnership, you will receive a K-1 statement having the details of your partnership's net income. Your share will then be taxed at the investor's individual tax rate.

One important note is that while the MLP's income is passed to you as a unit holder for tax purposes, the actual cash distributions made to you have little to do with the firm's income. Cash distributions are based on the MLP's distributable cash flow. Unlike dividends, these cash distributions are not taxed when they are received.

An advantage to investing in MLPs is that they have a much higher distributable cash flow when compared with taxable income. This is usually due to significant depreciation and other tax deductions associated with natural gas and oil companies – the most common businesses involved in an MLP structure.

Chapter 10
Ex Dividend Date

10
Ex Dividend Date

The ex-dividend date or reinvestment date is a term that involves payment of dividends on stocks of corporations and other financial holdings that are publicly and privately held.

According to IRS definition, the ex-dividend date is the first date (with respect to declaration) on which the stock buyer is not entitled to receive the next dividend payment.

You now know that a number of privately held and publicly traded companies pay dividends to their valid stockholders. However, the process of paying dividends can get a little bit complex as it is difficult to decide who will be paid. The composition of shareholders in most companies changes each day as stocks are being traded on a regular basis.

To make this process easier, companies declare a date, which is known as record date to pay dividends to the shareholders who own stocks on that day. However, paying dividends and clearing a stock purchase does take time. To compensate for this time, stock exchanges decide a date, generally two business days prior to the record date and this is what is known as ex-dividend date.

Interestingly, a stock's ex-dividend behavior is a source of confusion to most investors. They don't really know what happens to the market value of a stock if it goes "ex or ex-dividend". Here are some useful ideas to help you understand this concept better.

How Do Ex-Dividends Work?

Let's say there is a company called Zeal Inc. which trades on the stock exchange for $10 per share. The company has record earnings and its board of directors decides to pay a special extra dividend of $2 per share. Tuesday, April 23, 2013 is then set as the record date.

After reading through the first few lines, you know that the ex date will be two business days earlier, i.e. Friday, April 19, 2013.

If you own the company's stock on Thursday, April 18, 2013, you are entitled to receive the $2 dividend; however, if you wait to own the stock on Friday, April 19, 2013, you are not entitled to receive the dividend.

What Happens To the Stock's Value?

The question is what happens to the stock's value when the stock exchange closes on Thursday and then reopens on Friday. It is a bit difficult to assume the actual price drop as tax rates and rules differ for different buyers, but the price per share typically drops a few points.

Some More Details

Let's assume you bought 100 shares on Monday, April 15, 2013 for a settlement on Thursday, April 18, 2013 at a price of $10 per share. What happens next? Your stocks will go ex-dividend on Friday, April 19, 2013.

Since you are entitled to receive the dividend, you'll get a distribution of $2 x 100 = $200. Your check will be sent on Wednesday, April 24, 2013 (dividend checks are transferred only after the record date).

Additional Considerations for Mutual Funds

What should you do as an investor when buying mutual funds? Mutual funds also pay out profits to their shareholders and you need to find out when the fund is going to go "ex."

Chapter 11
Monthly Dividends and Quarterly Dividends

11
Monthly Dividends and Quarterly Dividends

Monthly Dividends

Some of you might be surprised to hear that there are stocks that pay you monthly dividends. Yes, they do exist! Of course there are stocks that pay dividends quarterly, semi-annually and yearly as well. Let's take a look at how stocks with monthly dividends can be a great addition to your investment portfolio.

Are Monthly Dividends Useful?

Well, there are a number of investors that jump into the 10-year US Treasury bond as it is considered one of the safest and most reliable investments. Sadly, these treasury bonds do not give you a yield of more than 2.2%.

Investment in the S&P 500, on the other hand, is also a popular option, but there is not a great deal of difference between the yields of US-treasury bond and S&P 500 stocks. However the question still remains, "how can I get a higher yield on my investment?"

Consider stocks that pay a monthly dividend when you want to increase yields on your investment.

What Are Monthly Dividend Stocks?

You know that there are stocks that pay dividends every quarter, so monthly dividends are not something out of the ordinary. Monthly dividend stocks are traded just like any other stock on a stock exchange and you can buy and sell them through your regular broker.

Most monthly dividend stocks belong to:

1. Oil and gas industry

2. Business development companies

3. Real Estate Investment Trusts or REITs.

How Are Monthly Dividend Stocks Different from Normal Stocks?

Most of you would like to know what exactly makes monthly dividend stocks different from other stocks. Well, these stocks generate their dividend payment from a number of different sources and streams of income. Monthly dividend stock payments are generated from corporate profits, rental income and interest payment on the underlying bonds that monthly dividend stocks invest in.

How Can Monthly Dividend Stocks Help You?

One of the prime reasons monthly dividend stocks are so popular is the fact that they help support income during retirement. You can also invest in monthly dividend stocks and compensate for your other high-risk investments (if any).

The best thing about monthly dividend stocks is that you can get higher yields, 8% or more, on many of these stocks. Much better than the yield you get on a 10-year U.S. Treasury Bond.

How You Can Search for Monthly Dividend Stocks?

Of course, you can find a few with Google search. You can also use an online tool such as Yahoo Finance's stock screener. All you have to do is enter the criteria you are looking for and don't forget to select a minimum of 8% yield under dividends. You can surely find a good number of stocks if you do your homework.

You also have an option to use websites that specialize in Dividend Stocks. These websites do the research for you, as well as give you the tools to make sound investment decisions.

Here are some websites to try.

www.DividendDetective.com

You can find the top 100 stocks based on yield, growth, cash flow, income, interest rate and payout ratio. The website also gives you the monthly dividend stock list, high dividends list, and the list of high return REIT's.

Another website which offers the same information, but charges for their subscription is www.DividendInvestor.com.

Can Monthly Dividend Stocks Fit in Your Portfolio?

You can earn high yields with monthly dividend stocks and all you have to do is treat them just like any other stock. Here is one important thing that you need to keep in mind.

If you are looking to build your wealth and increase your income, it is crucial that you have a bit of diversification in your monthly dividend stock investment. Since these stocks generate payments from specific sectors like real estate, oil and gas and mortgages, make sure that you are not too focused on any one specific sector.

You can always buy other stocks in the same sector if you don't want to be exposed to a great deal of individual stock risk. A good thing to do would be to keep your individual stock exposures to 1-3% and sector holdings to 10-15%. You can change your stock exposure and sector holdings after you have done research and analysis in the field.

Advantages of Investing in Monthly Dividend Stocks

Investing in monthly dividend stocks has become popular over the years and more and more investors are now getting in. Although you are probably more familiar with stocks that pay dividends quarterly (every 3 months), monthly dividend stocks are something new to many investors. Here are some benefits of investing in monthly dividend stocks.

1. You Get More Frequent Payments

If you don't want to invest in stocks that pay out dividends once a year or once a quarter, you can always put your money in a monthly dividend stock. Doing this will help you receive more dividend payments in a year when compared to investing in stocks that pay out dividends quarterly, semi-annually or annually.

Remember, if you want to ensure a steady stream of income by investing in stocks, try to add a variety of monthly dividend stocks as a valuable asset to your portfolio.

2. Monthly Dividend Stocks Take Advantage of Dollar Cost Averaging

Another great advantage of investing in monthly dividend stocks is the value of dollar cost averaging. You get a dividend payment every month and you can reinvest it to buy more stocks. This will definitely improve your portfolio as the number of shares you own will also increase. Over the passage of time, the value of stocks you own will potentially increase and this means you can get an impressive return on your overall investment.

Since your monthly dividend payment is calculated on a per-share basis, i.e. number of shares you own, you can use the payment you receive to buy more shares of monthly dividend stocks. Note that the more shares you own, the higher the monthly dividend payment you will receive. As you get larger payments, you can use the money to buy even more shares. Remember, buying more monthly shares has a snowball effect and your investment will build faster than many other methods that are available.

3. Monthly Dividend Stocks Are Often Less Volatile

If you are investing in monthly dividend stocks, you are often exposed to less volatility when compared to other stocks. This is because companies which pay out monthly dividends are set up differently from other corporations. A majority of the companies that offer monthly dividends are holding companies, trusts or REITs. They have a large portfolio of assets and income streams to generate revenue and pay out dividends.

Remember, if a company has a diversified portfolio, they can generate stable income regardless of the economic trends or other market factors. Traditional corporations on the other hand usually depend on one source of income; hence, can be affected by changing economic trends and market factors. When a traditional corporation suffers a setback, it cuts down on the dividends or eliminates dividend payments completely.

In addition to reduced payments, you may also notice big swings in stock prices. In the case of monthly dividends, stock prices tend to remain pretty steady and they generally increase over time. This gives you a chance to receive a nice return on your investment. Remember, you can use the steady dividend payment you get from monthly dividend stocks as you wish.

Quarterly Dividends

Investing in companies that pay dividends is one of the most popular ways to build wealth. As mentioned earlier, dividends are profits the company decides to distribute to its shareholders.

One important thing you need to keep in mind is that dividends do not represent all of the company's profits. Most companies retain some portion of dividends for future use, such as to get rid of debt.

You are most likely to receive dividends in the form of cash, but a company can also distribute dividends in the form of stocks. Having said all this, the company's board of directors is responsible to set the dividend rate that will be distributed to the shareholders. You also need to understand that a company can forego the dividend payment in case it is hurt financially or the board of directors is concerned about the company's future prospect.

If everything is going well, the company will pay you the dividend rate at a per share basis. For example, if the board of directors decides to pay a quarterly dividend of $0.50 per share and you have purchased 100 shares, you will receive $50 for that specific quarter.

Some Important Dates You Need to Remember

In case of dividends, there are 4 important dates that you need to remember.

Dividends Book

1. The Declaration Date

As the name suggests, this is the date the company's board of directors decides and announces that stockholders will receive their payment. The ex-dividend date is also announced along with the declaration date.

2. The Record Date

The record date is the date when the company finalizes the list of shareholders who will receive the dividend payment. You must be a valid stockholder before this date if you want to get the dividend.

3. The Ex-Dividend Date

As discussed in the previous chapter, the ex-dividend date falls 2 working days before the record date and this perhaps is the most important date as far as receiving the payment is concerned. Remember, even if you own the stocks after the ex-dividend date, you are not entitled to receive the payment. You can refer to the chapter on Ex-Dividend Dates to know more.

4. The Payment Date

This is the date when the company mails all the dividend checks or posts them to your brokerage account. If your goal is to make money and increase your wealth, you can invest in a company that has a good history of paying quarterly dividends.

Some More Advice on Quarterly Dividends

Since you have invested in a company, you get a part of the company's ownership and you will most likely be rewarded if your company does well. However, the company is free to set its own dividend payment schedule.

Another good thing about investing in stocks is that a company is more likely to increase the dividend payment than reduce it. The company's board of directors decides the dividend payment you will receive and most companies make quarterly distributions. Quarterly dividend means that you will receive the payment four times a year, i.e. after every 3 months. If a company decides to pay 8% of the share price annually, i.e. every year, then quarterly dividend payment will be divided into 4 equal parts. You will receive 2% of the share price as quarterly payments.

Why Should You Invest in Quarterly Dividend Stocks

Generally, companies that pay a quarterly dividend provide a steady income stream to the shareholders. More and more investors are attracted to buy stocks of companies that have a good payment history and as a result, these stocks sell at a higher price. Investing in stocks that provide quarterly dividends helps investors increase their income even after retirement.

Chapter 12
Stock Market Sectors

12
Stock Market Sectors

Investors normally use sectors to place stocks into different categories like technology, health care, energy, utility and telecommunication. Each stock market sector has unique characteristics as well as a different risk profile.

The word "sector" is commonly used to describe areas of economy in which businesses share the same products and services. Economies generally comprise of four different sectors.

The primary sector in an economy includes harvesting and extraction of natural products. You would find agriculture, mining and forestry industries in the primary sector.

The secondary sector in an economy includes businesses and industries involved in processing, manufacturing and construction.

The tertiary sector usually includes businesses that provide services such as entertainment, finance and retail sales. Quaternary sector is not commonly discussed but it includes intellectual businesses like education.

Why are Stocks Classified into Different Sectors?

Dividing sectors into different categories or sectors allows for more in-depth analysis of the stocks as a whole. It is common for stock market analysts and investors to specialize in particular stock market sectors.

Differences between an Industry and a Sector

Industry and sector are often used interchangeably to describe companies and businesses that operate in the same segment of the stock or economy or share similar characteristics. Even though the terms can be interchanged, they do have slightly different meanings.

The most obvious difference you can identify relates to their scope. Sectors normally refer to a large segment of the stock market or economy, while industry is normally used to describe a very specific group of companies.

The stock market can be broken down into a dozen of different sectors and each sector will feature companies that relate to the generalized business activity in that sector. Industries on the other hand are created when sectors are broken down into more specialized groupings.

Each of the dozen stock market sectors can have a varying number of companies and a single sector can feature even hundreds of companies.

For example, the banking sector in the stock market can be broken down into:

- Regional Northeast Banks

- Regional Mid-Atlantic Banks

- Regional Southeast Banks

- Foreign Regional Banks

- Money Center Banks

- Regional Midwest Banks

- Regional Pacific Banks

- Regional Southwest Banks

- Foreign Money Center Banks

Similarly, the Northwest regional **bank industry** will contain companies or banks that operate only in the Northwestern states.

When breaking down the stock market, you will first come across sectors that describe a general activity. Here is a list of general stock market sectors to give you a better idea.

Banking, capital goods, clothing, consumer durables, consumer non-durables, drugs, conglomerates, energy, financial, hardware, industrial goods, insurance, it services, medical facilities, consumer goods, construction, communications, technology, services, electronics, entertainment, credit, utilities, agriculture, chemicals, food and beverage, healthcare, investing, media, metals and mining, basic materials, software, media, real estate and transportation.

As you proceed, you'll see that companies that fall into a specific sector are categorized further where they are grouped with businesses that have very similar activities.

Stock Classification – Things You Need to Keep in Mind

One of the easiest ways to classify stocks is by the business type. Analysts and investors put stocks into different sectors for a better "comparison" and you often hear discussions about how certain "stock sectors" are performing.

In addition to the sector classification listed above, investors classify stocks as defensive or cyclical. Let's now have a closer look at both these categories and see how they appear to an individual investor.

Defensive Stocks

As the name suggests, defensive stocks are stable and provide constant dividends regardless of the current trends and state of the stock market.

* Take care not to confuse defensive stocks with defense stocks. The latter refers to buying stocks from companies that manufacture weapons, ammunition, fighter jets, etc.

Defensive stocks actually remain stable during the various phases of business cycles. Interestingly, defensive stocks perform better than cyclical stocks (more details later), especially when the market is experiencing recession. However, they tend to stay behind when the stock market is performing well.

The defensive stocks include consumer staples and utilities. Most investors typically invest in defensive stocks if they expect a stock market downturn. This is because regardless of the stock market conditions, people still need food, electricity and gas.

Another thing to keep in mind is that defensive stocks are a perfect choice to protect your portfolio when the stock market is falling. But, you should think about other choices when market conditions start improving. Defensive stocks do exactly what their name states and often fail to climb when market conditions get better.

Cyclical Stocks

Cyclical stocks as you can guess are largely affected by ups and downs in the stock market. These typically belong to companies that sell products or services that consumers can afford to buy when the economy is booming. Cyclical stocks rise with the rising business cycle, however, they can come crashing down during a recession.

For example, companies such as airlines, car manufacturers, furniture, hotel, clothing and retail are normally considered cyclical stocks. If the economy is doing well, the stock market will be booming because more and more people will be able to travel, renovate their homes, buy new cars or go shopping.

Similarly, if the economy is doing poorly, the first thing people cut out are unnecessary expenses on shopping and new cars. This means the value of cyclical stocks will go down and if the recession continues and is bad enough, the cyclical stocks can become completely worthless as the many "luxury" companies can go out of business.

Experts normally classify the following sectors as cyclical.

- Basic Materials
- Capital Goods
- Communications
- Consumer Cyclical
- Energy
- Financial
- Health Care
- Technology
- Transportation

Defensive or Cyclical – Which Stock is Better?

Investors do not have complete control over business cycles, but they can change and adjust their investing habits to make the most of the present economic situation. Your success as a stock investor depends on how well you understand the industries and your ability to sense the exact time when stocks are doing well.

We have discussed the basic definitions of defensive and cyclical stocks so that you can distinguish between the two. You already know that economic conditions can change without an indication so it is important that you are able to identify the areas that are best to invest your money in when the market starts to decline.

Defensive stocks are not affected as much by economic fluctuations and do well even when economic growth is really slow. If you invest in defensive stocks or commodities people always need (food, electricity, water or gas), your returns have a good chance of remaining constant.

Cyclical stocks perform well when people have lots of extra money to spend on luxuries. Identifying companies whose stocks are cyclical isn't a tough task. When the economy booms, companies dealing in car manufacturing, airlines, furniture, heavy machinery and expensive hotels tend to thrive. On the other hand, these companies are most likely to be wiped out of business when the market faces a downturn.

Given the unpredictable nature of the economy, how should you make your investment decisions?

The Concept of Cyclical and Defensive Stocks

Investing basics here are pretty simple as you only have to realize the difference between necessity and luxury. There are certain commodities you cannot live without so defensive stocks are guarded or defended against the adverse effects of a sour market.

For example, even if the stock market is not doing well, you would still buy toothpastes, shampoo, soap, detergents and bleach. People will still use water and electricity and cook their meals. Simply put, you cannot wait for the recession to go away before you buy shampoo or take a shower.

An excellent investment option when cyclical companies are suffering would be to put your money into a power or water supply company. By investing in a company that provides necessary services, you are less likely to see a drastic reduction in your returns.

Another attractive investment option for many investors are companies that provide fancy "necessary items." Still not sure about what this means? You cannot sacrifice deodorants, shampoos and bleach so companies like Procter & Gamble and Gillette are a good option even when the economy is in the dumps.

The Violent Nature of Cyclical Stocks

After reading through this chapter, you already know that cyclical stocks respond really quickly to economic changes. Companies dealing in cyclical stocks can suffer huge losses during recession and even fail to survive until the next boom. What's even more interesting is the fact that cyclical stocks can take a dramatic swing from profits to losses and there have also been instances where cyclical stocks have started doing well even before the economy comes out of recession.

Do Your Research and Get Your Investment Timing Right

Studies reveal that falling interest rates are one of the key factors behind the success of cyclical stocks. Since a reduction in interest rate stimulates economic growth, cyclical stocks are most likely to do well. On the other hand, the same cyclical stocks can perform poorly at a time when the interest rate is rising. While overall performance of cyclical stocks depends on interest rates, it is not the only factor that should influence your decision.

Before selecting a cyclical stock, it is important that you pick the safest companies. Bigger companies generally are safer compared to high risk smaller companies, but the latter is more likely to give you impressive returns.

You also need to understand that correct investment timings are different for different cyclical sectors. For example, paper, cement and petrochemical industries tend to move first. Once economic recovery looks certain, technology stocks start to flow. Other companies such as clothing stores, airline and car manufacturers join in at the end.

Simply put, businesses are more likely to expand when economic times are good. Companies buy building materials and equipment to build and expand their facilities so equipment, technology, heavy machinery and construction are cyclical stocks. Cyclical stocks such as steel manufacturing rise significantly when companies make purchases to expand their business.

You shouldn't rely on cyclical stocks if you are looking for long-term gains. If you sense that the present economic condition will deteriorate further, try to unload cyclical stocks before their prices fall. Remember, if you remain stuck with lots of cyclical stocks during recession, you might have to wait for a long time (5 years, 10 years or maybe more) before the cyclical stocks return to the lucrative value they once had.

Just like any sport, investment in stocks is all about finding the right combination of aggressiveness and defense, most importantly at the right time. You cannot find success with a single tactic, therefore, both defensive and cyclical stocks should be part of your investment portfolio. Another thing you need to pay attention to is the proportion of defensive and cyclical stocks in your investment portfolio.

If the market looks bad, try to move towards defensive stocks and stay from cyclical stocks. Remember:

1. Cyclical stocks can move dramatically (i.e. can rise and fall) with changes in the business cycle, while defensive stocks show little movement in response to business cycles.

2. Cyclical stocks are products and services you buy when the economy is booming and defensive stocks are products and services you cannot ignore regardless of the state of the economy.

Investing in the Stock Market – What You Need to Know

Investing in the stock market without a doubt is scary for most novice investors. There are endless choices and some quite lucrative ones as well, but even one step in the wrong direction can result in huge losses. And, this is exactly what most investors never want to experience.

The stock market is certainly not the safest, but this does not mean you put off your investment plans and never get started. Remember, today is the best time to start and procrastinating or shying away from your fears can never help you succeed. If you have a preset idea in mind, you can always reach your goals.

First of all, here's something you need to keep in mind. There is no definite set of rules when it comes to deciding the minimum amount you need to invest. You can always customize your portfolio and your investment amount to meet your objectives. The stock market on the other hand allows you to customize your portfolio and meet your objectives. Most importantly, you can achieve a diversified portfolio without investing in a lot of individual securities.

If you've just started investing in the stock market, it is better if you invest in leading companies in different stock market sectors. The company you select should have a strong balance sheet, i.e. lots of cash with very low debt. Most novice investors, as well as experts, prefer to put their money in companies that have a strong history of growing sales, increased earnings and steady dividends.

You are likely to make more gains when you invest in companies that have been in business for a long time and continue to progress despite the crises situation.

Strong companies should form the core of your portfolio, and you can always add more companies and stocks to diversify your portfolio further. Remember, customized portfolios give better performances as you can adapt them to meet your objectives easily.

Successful investing tactics can differ slightly when you are young and when you retire. For example, if you have graduated recently, you are prepared to embark on your dream career, which hopefully will be very successful. Since you are working and have steady cash flow, you can invest aggressively and build your wealth.

On the other hand, when you retire, you need to preserve your money and build it very carefully, so you can say that retirees need to have a more conservative approach. So whether you want to enjoy your retirement days or benefit from your career, you should definitely go for diversification in your portfolio.

This is because if you invest in a few stocks, one bad performance can ruin all your hard work and your gains will be in jeopardy. If you have a variety of stocks, you can manage your gains and still be able to survive a setback.

As a new entry into the stock market, it is better to invest in a maximum of 12 stocks and then slowly increase the number so you can keep up on each and every stock.

Not only should you select stocks from different sectors, you should also look to diversify your holdings in other categories such as risk, size, local (U.S.) or foreign, and most importantly types such as cyclical, defensive or speculative. Needless to say, take care that you don't become severely overweight in any one category.

Quick Recap: Importance of Stock Market Research, Evaluation and Industry Analysis

One of the reasons most people are scared of the stock market is that it is a tough battle of the mind. Of course, you have to keep track of numbers, research better prospects and perform industry analysis. And, all these are really important.

Before you head to an industry pundit or analyst, keep one thing in mind. If you are putting money on the line, buying and selling stocks is most likely to become an emotional thing. You can experience fear when your stock goes down on earnings and become overconfident when you get a good run of profits. Some investors can become really emotional and depressed after a string of losses.

Since you have decided to enter the stock market, how well you handle your emotions actually decides how much money you will make. Your reflexes should be really sharp and investors that react promptly when the stock does poorly are usually the ones that excel. Remember, you need to have a well thought out plan to keep pace with the changing stock market.

Dividends Book

Here's a quick recap about what we've discussed in this particular chapter and how you can take full advantage of what the stock market has to offer.

1. Investing in the stock market is a great way to build your wealth. You will be really happy with the money you make regardless of the amount you invest.

2. Try not to invest too much money in one particular stock. This way you limit your options and if that stock goes into a free fall, you are less likely to suffer. Having a diversified portfolio ensures that your overall risk is greatly reduced.

3. Don't forget to have another look at your stock portfolio every few months as the stock market and economic conditions change constantly. Your portfolio should always fit the investment model that will give you maximum gains. Another thing you must consider is that some stock sectors might do better than others for some time, but fail to perform later.

    Depending upon the conditions, certain companies will show exceptional growth while some might be wiped out of the picture. Therefore, it is crucial that you adjust your portfolio as needed and secure your investment.

4. If you've just started out, never invest more than you can afford to lose. This becomes especially important if your portfolio has high risk investments. Another important thing to remember is that so-called "safe investments" are not entirely RISK FREE.

Yes, all investments carry a certain risk depending on their nature, so put your money into investments that carry lower risks.

5. You cannot afford to be short-sighted when investing in the stock market. Remember, the market is extremely volatile and if you make short-term plans, you are not likely to build wealth. Making a long-term investment plan gives you a better chance of seeing positive returns, so carefully decide the time when you want to buy and sell stocks. Moreover, you need to set realistic goals in order to achieve the most success in the stock market.

6. Don't allow your money to remain in a stock(s) that is not benefiting you. Remember, stock market decisions should be made wisely and there is no room for emotions. Even if you love a particular company but its stock is continuously losing, there's no point in holding on to it.

7. You should treat your stocks as if they are your own company.

    Make sure you take time to look over the company's finance statements as well as review its strengths and weaknesses. Once you have a clear idea about the leading companies in the stock market, you can wisely decide the stocks you should purchase.

8. Seasoned investors do a smart thing, i.e. they search for valuable stocks that others do not want. Expert investors know how they can make gains by investing into companies that no one cares about. Even though it is risky, it can pay off. The key here is to search for companies

Dividends Book

that offer stocks that are most likely to perform really well. Remember, if you do your research, you can find diamonds.

9. Don't ever invest in a company's stock if you haven't thoroughly researched it. Jumping blindly into the market increases your chances of suffering badly because if the company isn't successful, you will lose money.

Chapter 13
Risk and Reward

13
Risk and Reward

We all hear that there is no investment that is without risk and you need to consider the right things with a long-term view before investing. There are "safe" investments as well, which means there is low risk.

After reading through the first few pages of the Book, you know that all investors need to accept a certain amount of risk to build wealth over time. Think about it. If you leave your money in a risk-free environment such as a low return bank savings account, you are not "investing" anything at all.

Since you are taking on very little risk, keeping a significant portion of your assets in the savings account even for years does not give you high returns. What's even more alarming is the fact that you might lose your purchasing power over the long period of time as the prices of goods are constantly rising.

So, if you want to create more wealth, you will need to grow it rather than just preserve it. The steps you need to take depend on your long-term goals and you'll have to consider "riskier" investment options than a bank savings account.

If you take a closer look at the investment options, you'll find that there are low risk investments and there are some complex options with risky financial moves as well. The latter is more appropriate for expert and professional investors.

If you have ever had a chance to invest in a 401(k) plan, you will be familiar with risk profiling. 401(k) managers allow you to select your investment and retirement portfolio based on how much risk you can afford. You'll have to answer a few questions and based on your answers, you (the investor) will be categorized into different risk tolerance levels; usually low, medium, and high.

Measuring and Evaluating Risks in Any Investment

Measuring and evaluating the risk involved in your investment is a little complex. There are several elements you need to consider and evaluating the different types of risk that can affect your investment is critical to knowing which investment is most appropriate for you.

How You Can Define 'Risk'

Risk is the chance that your actual return will be different from what you expect, with a possibility that you lose some or all of your original investment. Risk is measured by calculating the standard deviation of the return of a specific investment. If you get a high standard deviation, your investment carries a high degree of risk.

You will be amazed to know that most companies hire specialized personnel and allocate large amounts of money to manage the risk associated with their business and most importantly, their business dealings (investment). One term you will hear quite often is "risk assessment" and it involves assessing the risk surrounding a specific business or investment.

One of the basic ideas in investment is the relationship between risk and return. Generally, if you are willing to take more risk, you are most likely to get greater returns. The basic reason behind this statement is that as an investor, you must be appreciated and compensated for taking on additional risk.

Here's an example to help you understand better. You invest in a U.S. Treasury bond, which is considered to be one of the safest investments. Since it is believed to be risk free, it gives a lower return when compared to other risky investments such as a corporate bond.

The major reason for this difference is that the corporation, which issues the corporate bond, is more likely to go bankrupt than the U.S. government. Because you are willing to take the additional risk by investing in a corporate bond, you are offered a higher and better rate of return.

Different Types of Risks

Market Risk

Market risk defines the possibility for you as an investor to experience losses due to factors that have an impact on the overall performance of the financial markets.

For example, if you are invested in stocks or stock-based index funds, the overall economic condition of your state, country and even the world, will have an influence on your investment's value and cause it to fluctuate. Market risk can be applied to investments in single companies and even bonds.

You also have to understand that the performance of your investment is also related to a market crash. Even if your investment quality remains the same, you will get lower return when there is a market crash or decline.

Market risk is also crucial for investments that follow strong trends.

For example, there are times when real estate appears to be a good investment and your property value will go up. Similarly, if people start believing that your investment (real estate property) is overly priced, it could lose value even though it hasn't changed a bit physically.

Default Risk

Default risk is mostly related to the quality of your core investment and it becomes more important when you are investing (through stocks or bonds) in a single company. The moment you invest in a company's stock, you expect a guaranteed return, but there is a default risk. You will not receive the return you were promised if the company goes bankrupt.

Pensions, which are thought to be one of the most stable incomes for retirees, are also exposed to default risk. The promised benefit might disappear or reduce if your company restructures later.

Interest Rate Risk

Interest rate risk, as the name suggests is the possibility that your investment will decline in value when interest rate rises. This risk is mostly applicable to securities that offer a fixed rate of return. You expose yourself to interest rate risk when you buy bonds and preferred stocks.

Liquidity Risk

Liquidity risk defines the possibility that you may not be able to buy or sell your investment in sufficient quantities when desired, because your options are limited.

A perfect example to understand liquidity risk is selling real estate. It might not be easy to buy or sell a property at any given time. This is very different when compared with government securities or blue-chip stocks.

The 'Risk/Reward Ratio'

The Risk/Reward ratio is used by most investors to compare their expected returns of an investment with the amount of risk associated with them. You can calculate this ratio by dividing the amount of money you can lose if the price moves in the unexpected direction (i.e. your risk) by the amount of profit you are expected to make when the position is closed (your reward).

You can calculate the "risk/reward" ratio to decide whether or not it is beneficial to take the pain. Remember, understanding the relationship between risk and reward is very crucial in building your investment portfolio.

As we've discussed on a couple of occasions, all investment have carry risk to a certain degree. And the rule you have to remember is that "the higher the risk, higher will be your returns."

Having said this, there's an additional consideration. Before you start picking high-risk investments, you must know where your comfort level is and how much risk you can easily afford.

How Much Money Can You Lose?

One of the most common questions among beginners is "how much money am I likely to lose?"

Of course, this statement is quite important, but it only covers one side of your investment picture. If you are evaluating risk/reward ratio or any investment for that matter,

1. Figure out whether or not your "investment", i.e. the principal amount is going to lose money.

2. You also need to figure out whether or not you will be able to achieve your investment goal. This is especially important if you are investing to enjoy your retirement.

3. Another important thing to consider is whether or not you are willing to take additional risk to boost your return.

The scariest thing about investment is the danger that your investment will lose money, i.e. your principal amount might reduce. However, there are investments that guarantee that your principal amount will remain unaffected. These are convenient, but you are less likely to make higher gains.

For example, U.S. Treasury bonds are the safest in the world, however, you have to pay the price for safety, which is getting a very low return on your investment. If you calculate your net gain after deducting inflation and taxes you pay, you surely won't be impressed by the real growth in your wealth.

Many investors are willing to accept the risk in their investments if they are able to achieve their investment goals. Before you evaluate the risk/reward ratio, you need to keep a close eye on:

1. The total amount of money you've invested

2. The length of time you've invested

3. Rate of return

4. Taxes, inflation and other deductions

If you are not willing to take on additional risk in your investments, you can compensate your lower returns by increasing the principal amount and the total time of investment. Another thing you can try is diversifying your portfolio and holding investments having varying degrees of risk. This way, you can benefit from the booming market as well as protect yourself from dramatic losses if the market goes down.

What is Your Comfort Level?

As an investor, you need to find your own comfort level with risk and create a portfolio based on that very return. Remember, if your portfolio carries greater risk, there is a potential for exceptional returns, but there are equal chances of failing significantly.

The best thing to do in a situation like this is to stick to the amount of risk which doesn't hinder your "good night's sleep."

Interestingly, there is no "ideal", "right" or "wrong" amount of risk, and the choice is solely your personal decision. If you are young and have a job, you can go ahead and take higher risks as you have more chances to recover from a disaster when compared with older investors.

If you are nearing retirement or want to prepare for it, it is better if you don't take extraordinary risks as there will be very little time to recover from a significant loss. However, having a "too conservative approach" at this stage is also not recommended as you will have a hard time achieving your financial goals.

How You Can Take Control of Your Risk/Reward Ratio

You can control the risk in your portfolio to a certain degree by having a proper mix of stocks and bonds. Experts believe that portfolios that are heavily geared toward stocks are riskier when compared to a portfolio that favors bonds. You are the best person to judge the amount of risk you can afford, so find your comfort level and build your portfolio accordingly

Chapter 14
My Dad's Retirement Plan

14
My Dad's Retirement Plan

When it comes to investing your money, the best thing you can do is create a plan. Sit down and think before you choose any investment. Remember, your hard work will be extremely useful in shaping your investments in the future.

As we've discussed earlier, the key to any investment is thorough preparation and research. Before you jump into every attractive offer, it is better if you get an accurate picture of your current financial situation. Take time to see what you own, how much you owe and what your income and expenditure are.

Your Game Plan – Setting up Investment Goals

Like every other plan, you need to set and confirm your investment plan goals. I idolized my dad from a young age and will share some of his investment secrets later in this section. You can find his "successful" investment plan under the section titled "The Ten Commandments." Ultimately, the biggest secret in the investment world is this. "Don't complicate things for yourself and stick to your plan."

Now back to our discussion on goals and objectives. The goals and objectives you set become the backbone of your investment plan. Once you determine what you want to achieve, you can easily decide how much risk you are willing to take to achieve those goals. The previous chapter on risk and reward will definitely help you with this.

Your investment strategy is more likely to be successful when you have both short-term and long-term goals. For example, your short-term investment goal could be to buy a house within 2 years and a long-term goal could be to build a portfolio that will help you generate income for use during retirement years. Remember, knowing what you want to achieve will definitely make it easier to customize the investment plan to fit your requirements.

Once you determine your goals, the next step is to decide how much money you can initially use for investment. Remember, you need to have at least the same or slightly higher amount of money set aside as a backup. You surely don't want to see all your money sinking directly in a bad investment.

Planning Your Investment Amount

Planning your investment can be tricky especially if you don't know where to start. Let's say you want to have enough money to enjoy your retirement. Everyone dreams about retiring comfortably, so your plan needs to be more specific. Instead of saying that you want to enjoy your retirement, think about exactly how much money you want to save. You can set specific and realistic goals such as "save $600,000 by the time I reach 65."

Once you decide the amount, you need to calculate how much you'll need to save each month. Again, this amount should be realistic and most importantly, achievable using your investment strategy. If you are not able to set the fixed amount aside each month, it is time to readjust your financial goals and investment plan.

Choosing Your Investment Strategy

You can go for an aggressive investment strategy such as high-risk investments if you're saving for long-term goals and can afford to lose money when markets fluctuate. On the other hand, low-risk or rather conservative investments are not a bad option either. The best thing to do here would be to go for a more "balanced" approach, i.e. the right mix of high-risk and low-risk investment.

Stick to Your Investment Plan

You need to follow the rules and guidelines you've outlined in your investment plan to get the most of your portfolio. Simply put, your investment plan should:

1. Define your investment goals and objectives clearly.

2. Describe the strategies that will help you achieve your goals.

3. Indentify expected returns and the time frame required to achieve those returns.

4. Define the risk you're willing to take.

Dividends Book

5. Indentify the different types of investments that will make up your portfolio.

6. Specify how you will monitor your portfolio and when and how you will readjust it.

Quick Reminder – What is Your Tolerance Level for Investment Risk?

Different combinations of investments may work best for you, but before you select investment classes, it is important that you are willing to take the amount of risk associated with the particular investment. Remember, you need to be comfortable with the risk as you'll have to face the potential consequences of your important investment decisions.

A variety of factors can influence your overall risk tolerance including:

1. Your short-term and long-term financial goals

2. The main reason(s) you've decided to invest

3. Your expected returns

4. How long you plan to keep your money locked in an investment i.e. Time Horizon

5. Whether or not you want to access your money quickly

6. Your knowledge of the investment market

7. How you react after a sudden increase or decrease in the value of your investment(s)

One thing to keep in mind is that your risk tolerance can change as you become experienced and confident with investing. If you are not sure about investment types that suit you, there are a number of online tools that can help you make a better decision.

Some investors are tempted to sell their investments when the market falls in value with an intention to buy back later. This approach may look sensible considering the scenario, but closer examination reveals that it can be quite risky. The main reason is that markets continue to rise and fall in value all the time, so it is hard to time getting out and when to get back in.

If you are trying to shield yourself from the adverse effects, you may be tempted to take advantage of short-term fluctuation, i.e. sell when the market is hitting a low. However, you need to remember that it is the time you spend in the market, not accurate timings that determines the amount of wealth you can ultimately create.

We have talked a lot about evaluating risk you can tolerate easily and this is especially important in context to your investment plan.

Think about it. If you have a number of high-risk investments in your portfolio, you can grow your wealth faster, but there is an equal chance of losing some or all of your money. Before you pick up a large number of high-risk investments for your portfolio, ask yourself a simple question. "Am I comfortable taking on lots of risk to get greater returns?"

Remember, you have to be comfortable taking on risk as it is not easy to make a decision when you don't know whether or not your money will be there when you need it the most.

Another simple thing you need to be very clear about is how much money you expect to make on your investment. It is vital to keep track of the return you make on every investment to know whether or not you will reach your financial goals.

Even though the statement sounds needless, you might need to change your goals and of course, the amount of "expected returns" if you're not comfortable with taking on more risk than what you can easily afford. Just recall what we've discussed in the previous chapter. To get more returns, you often need to take more risks.

How long you plan to invest for is another important thing you need to keep in mind. Your investment **time horizon** is the amount of time you need to invest your money to meet your goals. The time period for which you hold on to an investment is your personal choice and it can range from 6 months to as long as 20 years (such as the case in retirement).

The time horizon is also an important factor in choosing investments that will make up your portfolio. For example, if you only have short-term plans, you can go with "conservative" low-risk investments that guarantee return. This way your money will be safe and with you when you need it. And, if you have long-term plans, you can always choose "riskier" investments.

Liquidity is something you need to consider if you want quick access to your money. Liquidity defines how easy it is to "free" your money from an investment. Bank accounts and cash have higher "liquidity" and you can get your money back right away and most importantly, very easily. However, these options offer low returns.

You can now see that investments that are less liquid offer higher returns, but they come with more risk.

Who Is My Dad, And Why Should You Listen To Him?

Let me tell you a little bit about my Dad. My father spent many years climbing the corporate ladder, then later in his career became a very successful small business owner.

He never taught at a university or college...

He wasn't on any Presidential Advisory Committees...

He didn't hob-nob with the "economic elite" at K-Street parties (the same "elite" now sandbagging our total economy!)

What he did know was that NO ONE cares about your money more than you!

He was – and still is – a virtual genius at squeezing the last drop of profit he can from his investment portfolio. In fact, one longtime friend of mine, a much respected business professor, said my Dad was one of the smartest businessmen he has ever seen regarding investments.

For over 30 years my Dad has used his system – **averaging double digit returns** the entire time. His method has produced an excellent income stream - without touching his principle - in both good markets and in bad.

It's said that those who can – do. Those that can't – teach. My Dad's techniques speak for themselves.

This method is sound, tried and true – and works in the real world of mortgages, car payments and supporting a family.

Pragmatic, Down to Earth, Actionable Information!

I am constantly in awe at how my Dad is able to **see through the smoke, mirrors and drivel** almost every talking head, financial pundit, and our hopelessly clueless press are passing around as "sound" investment advice.

The Ten Commandments – My Dad's Retirement Plan

One: Keep it Simple

As you make investment plans for the future, here's the single best tip my dad has to offer. Keep your investing strategy simple and don't complicate things for yourself.

The best way to avoid pitfalls in investing is to stick to your plan and be in close contact with your goals. Your investment goals need to be simple so that you know the exact point you need to change them.

Two: Use the Millionaire's Secret

As My Dad always says, "Who knows better how to preserve wealth and multiply it than the Rockefeller's, Walton's, Dupont's, and Mellon's." As you recall we discussed in Chapter One how these families' wealth is invested in company stocks that pay consistently increasing dividends.

Three: Use the DRIP with the Roth IRA

Let us see how powerful this is. If you invest $5,000 per year at age 29, in a Roth IRA until you are age 65, and assuming it averages 9 percent per year, your investment will be worth $1,286,880.

Yes, you will be a millionaire, and your withdrawals will be tax free. The best part is you will make 25 percent on your money per year just by being tax free, assuming you are in the average middle income tax bracket, plus your 9 percent. Yes this is completely legal, and approved by our government.

You can see why the Roth IRA is the best retirement plan for most people. Always consult your tax professional to be sure it is the best for you.

Four: Diversify into 8 to 10 Stock Market Sectors

After reading through the previous chapter and the earlier discussion, you know that risk is an inherent part of investing and you can't avoid it. However, you can manage it in a variety of different ways and diversification is one of the key strategies. Investors have used diversification over the years to reduce their investment risk.

Diversification involves spreading your money across a number of different investments depending on factors such as your short-term and long-term goals, amount you want to invest and the risk you are willing to take on comfortably. This strategy is useful considering the fact that every investment has its own pros and cons. The market can go up and down and this movement does have an impact on your investment.

When you own a diverse range of investments such as stocks, you can easily achieve investment returns in a convenient and consistent manner.

Most of you will have one question, "what is the best way to diversify?"

Well, the more you diversify, the more you can reduce your investment risk. The best way you can diversify includes:

1. Investing across different asset classes such as property, shares and cash

2. Having more than one investment within each type. For example you can invest in different industries and companies offering shares.

3. If you are investing in a fund, a great way to diversify is investing in more than one type of fund.

Five: Choose a Risk you are Comfortable With

This perhaps is the most important factor that determines your success as an investor. You need to look at investment risk and return before you set your expectations. Remember, the amount of risk associated with an investment largely determines your asset allocation. Most investors outline the risk they are willing to accept before they create their investment portfolio.

If you are investing for the first time, it is important that you have a specific goal in mind. Figure out your expected return and then decide the investments you'll pick for your portfolio for the specific time period. The statement does sound funny, but no investor can accurately guess the actual returns before they invest. You can go with a prediction and estimate an expected return – something that'll help you readjust your goals and portfolio later. You can review your expected return weekly, monthly or annually and make relevant changes to your portfolio.

Here are some observations to help you understand the relationship between risk and expected return.

An expected annual return of 3% to 6% is likely to be the result of a well-diversified portfolio with low-risk investment.

An expected annual return of 7% to 12% is likely to be the result of a well-diversified portfolio with moderate-risk investment.

An expected annual return of 13% to 19% is likely to be the result of a well-diversified portfolio with higher-risk investment.

An above 20% return with a diversified portfolio a high risk investment.

Your expected returns on investment should be determined for two different periods of time, i.e. before retirement and during retirement. You can estimate your expected returns over a period of time by looking at the performance of the asset class you've selected.

Since you have to accept more risks to get a higher return, we come back to the same question. "What is your **risk-tolerance level** or how much risk are you willing to accept?"

The answer to this question is quite simple. Your age and stage in your life influences the amount of risk you are willing to take. If you are young, you are more willing to accept more risk because you have more time to bounce back from a setback. You can overcome losses and there is more time to grow your portfolio and of course, your total wealth.

As you grow older, you don't have as much time to experiment as you will need your wealth sooner after retirement. Generally, older investors have lower risk tolerance and the majority of people invest in bonds and cash as these investments carry minimum risk when compared to other asset classes. On the flip side, having a portfolio that is heavily dependent on bonds and cash will give you lower returns.

The biggest challenge of investing successfully is to balance your risk and expected return keeping in mind your personal goals. If you want to make more money, you can try buying U.S. and international stocks rather than putting all your money in bonds and cash.

Six: Pick 8-10 Stocks that You Manage.

No one manages your money better than you. Your stockbroker is working just like you to sell what his company wants him to sell you. This book will empower you to make smart decisions, so you can accomplish your goals.

When it comes to making money and accumulating wealth, only few investments are talked about as much as stocks are.

The next chapter summarizes some of the most popular strategies used by investors for picking good stock. A few of them also tell you how you can avoid the bad ones. In short, you need to focus on the art of stock-picking and select 8 to 10 stocks based on a certain set of criteria I will discuss later. Your aim in stock picking should be to select quality stocks which give you a higher rate of return than other average stocks.

So why is stock-picking so important? Well, there should be some reason why investors worry so much about picking stocks and spend hours reviewing their choices. The answer is obvious – lots of money. When you become a good stock-picker, you can increase your return and personal wealth exponentially.

More details on stock-picking are coming up in the next chapter.

Seven: Take a Profit When Stock is Up Ten Percent

When a stock is up ten percent over what you have purchased it at it is advised to take a profit. You can wait longer, but you will need to keep a close eye so that it does not fall below your target profit price. If for example you bought your stock at $30, and it goes up over the year to $35 you may want to sell and take your profit. You will hit your target ten percent profit when the stock hits $33. You will realize this gain of 16.66 percent plus your interest for the year. If it pays ten percent interest your gain would be 26.66 percent for the year.

Eight: No Stock on Margins

Never ever buy stock on Margins. When you buy Stock on Margins you are buying a security such as stock by borrowing money from your broker. As an example you buy a number of shares of a stock for $10,000 dollars. You put down $2,000 dollars, and your broker lends you the $8,000 dollars. He is securing your loan with the stock you have in your account. The idea is if the stock goes up you sell, and make a profit. If the stock goes down you lose, and have to start selling your other stocks to pay off the loan difference of loss. It is very risky, and you could lose everything very quickly.

Nine: When Buying Look at High and Low over the Last Year Never pay more Than 60 percent of high for previous year.

When you buy a stock you always want to look at the high and low over the last year. You can go to Yahoo.com's finance section and type in the symbol of the company you want to buy. It will take you to the research page on the stock. It will have the high and low posted over the last 52 weeks. Let us look at an example. A telephone company, Windstream Corporation has the ticker symbol (WIN). The research shows the stock over the last 52 weeks has a low of $7.78 and a high of $11.04 and currently is selling at $7.94/share and pays a dividend of 12.6 percent. I see the price is almost at the lowest it has been in a year, so this is one I want to do further research on, seeing if it meets my risk level, and qualifies based on past performance of dividend payment. See the next Chapter for more information on this.

Ten: Only Buy Companies Making a Profit That Pay Dividends

Before you start investing in a company, it is vital that you get familiar with the company's business as well as its products or services. More than anything else, you need to find out whether or not your desired company is making money and if the company is losing money, you need to find out the exact reasons why.

What should you look for in a company?

The most obvious factor is the company's financial performance. How well a company manages its finances says a lot about how it will handle stocks, stock market changes as well as unexpected events. Here are some questions that can help you assess a company's financial standing.

- Has the company's business been up or down in recent years?

- Is the company really making money and investing wisely in its future?

- If the company is doing poorly, is there chance of improvement in the near term?

- Will the company issue new shares when they are losing money?

- Does the company have enough assets to cope with short-term debt or adverse events?

- If the company falls short of cash, how will it repay its debt?

The answers to these questions depend on the company's track record. If the company shows steady growth in the market, there is a chance it is making money. Remember, share prices of companies with a good track record are more likely to increase when compared to share prices of companies with no or poor track records. Take care to look at the financial statements and prospectus of a company carefully before investing.

It is not always easy to find company history or financial details especially if the company is privately held. This is because private companies cannot disclose financial details about their business activities. If you want to invest in a private company, you can directly ask the company for the information you need.

Another thing you need to look at in a company is its leadership. If a company has good leaders or the management hasn't changed often, it proves that the company management is stable and you are likely to make more gains by investing in their shares.

Perhaps the most important factors you need to consider are the company's intention about future growth and dividend history. Investing in companies with a good dividend history means you have more chances of a steady income.

Chapter 15
How to Choose a Dividend Stock: Past Performance is Usually a Good Indicator

15
How to Choose a Dividend Stock: Past Performance is Usually a Good Indicator

Let's say you want to invest some money and buy the best stocks you can. Most people, particularly those who are nearing retirement are more likely to turn to dividend paying stocks to create a steady source of income. The bottom line is that there is no one ideal way to pick stocks and every stock strategy depends largely on the best guess.

You have hundreds of stocks to choose from and you surely want to accumulate wealth by investing in stocks. Interestingly, when it comes to personal finance or investment for retirement, not many subjects are as popular as stocks. And, it is quite easy to figure out the reason. The stock market is thrilling and most investors want to experience the ups without the downs on this exciting roller-coaster ride.

In this particular section, we look at some of the most popular strategies for finding the best stocks. Now, before we explore the details of stock-picking, it is important to note that there is no infallible strategy to select stocks. Yes, unfortunately, investing in the stock market has no magical rules, but there are formulas that guarantee success.

Now back to our discussion on the art of stock-picking. You can expand your wealth through the stock market, but here are pointers you need to keep in mind when deciding the stocks you should pick.

1. A number of factors represent a company's financial health so you cannot construct one formula to work with. Information such as total profits is easy to find, but you cannot really determine factors such as competitive advantage and company reputation.

2. The stock market can change unpredictably and stocks don't always perform the way you anticipate. Emotions in the stock market frequently change and this is the exact reason the stock market is such a volatile place.

At this time, you might be asking this question – "why should I worry about the way I pick stocks?"

The answer is simple. You should pick your stocks carefully if you want to create wealth. Stock picking is as important as creating an investment plan because you want the stocks to help you achieve your financial goals. Now that you are familiar with the reason why you should devote time to picking stocks, let's continue to the most popular strategies of stock picking.

Fundamental Analysis

You might hear that a company has strong fundamentals and you need to invest in it. Well, any person can easily understand what fundamentals are and why they should be analyzed. Remember, fundamental analysis is a great point to start when picking good stocks.

Doing basic fundamental evaluation for stocks is quite straightforward. All you have to do is find a stock's intrinsic value, i.e. value you believe a stock is really worth. If a stock's intrinsic value is more than the current market price, it is sensible to go ahead with the deal, i.e. buy stocks.

Qualitative Analysis

Stock picking is not all about number crunching, but you do need to look at the qualitative factors of a company before picking stocks.

Basically, you need to invest in a reputable company and the backbone of any successful company is strong management. When people at the top are competent, they make better decisions when determining the fate of the company. You can also do some research and find out about the management of the company.

You will also need to see how well the business is run in an open and transparent way. If the management has the qualities you believe are essential for success, you can think about investing.

Another important thing you need to consider before picking company stocks is how it makes money. If you reframe this question, it would become "what is the company's business model?"

Remember, having know-how of company activities will be profitable in the long run as you will know whether or not their stocks will be in demand. In addition to company activities, you need a solid understanding of how the company generates income.

Moreover, you need to identify the growth potential of a company. For example, a reputable company in an industry that is in great demand will offer a solid return when compared to a mediocre company in an industry that has no growth potential.

It is always better to invest in companies that have a valuable brand when you are starting out. For example, if you invest in large corporations like Proctor & Gamble, you actually increase your chances of making solid gains. This is because P&G has hundreds of popular brands like Head & Shoulders and Tide and the good performance of one brand can easily compensate for average performance of any other brand.

Well, if all this information is confusing you, there is nothing to worry about. You don't have to be a finance guru to recognize a company that will do well. If you see a company that is expanding and belongs to an industry that is booming, dig a little deeper and who knows, it might become the next big thing in the stock market. This strategy looks really simple, but it is one of the most effective ways to evaluate a potential investment.

Value Investing

Value investing is one of the most widely used stock picking methods. A value investor picks stocks based on earnings, dividends, book value and cash flow. They pick companies that are undervalued by the market (i.e. have a lower price) and have the potential to increase in value later.

Since we are not going into the details of value investing, you only need to keep one thing in mind. Value investing does not mean buying every stock that declines with an intention that the share price will increase when the market gets better. You have to be confident that you are picking a company that is "high quality" at a relatively low price. Remember, you should learn to distinguish between a valuable "cheap" company and a mediocre company that has a declining price.

Growth Investing

Growth investing has yielded extraordinary returns for investors but before you jump onto the growth investing bandwagon, it is important to know that this strategy has substantial risks and not everyone can benefit from it.

Growth investing works in contrast with value investing. If value investors pick stocks that are trading for less than their intrinsic value, growth investors on the other hand go for stocks that are trading for more than their intrinsic value.

The reason growth investors go for such stocks is that they believe the company's intrinsic worth will grow and the stock prices will increase further. You can say that growth investors are more concerned with a company's future growth. When there is an increase in company earnings and revenue, it will directly translate into an increase in stock prices.

The best way to pick stocks using this strategy is by investing in companies that belong to the rapidly expanding industry sector. You can invest in new companies that relate to new technology with an intention that they'll make huge profits.

Like any other stock picking strategy, there is no absolute formula for growth investing. Every strategy or method of stock picking requires interpretation and judgment and you can use your own rules for growth investing. Specifically, you must consider the growth potential of a company as well as its industry's performance. Here are some additional points to consider.

Strong Earnings

One of the most important questions a growth investor should ask is whether or not the company's revenue has been growing. The basic concept is that if the company has displayed good growth in the past, it is more likely to grow in the coming years.

Excellent Management

The company's management also has an important role to play in increasing the company's overall gains and profits. If a company shows high annual revenue growth, it is more likely a good candidate to invest in.

If you're looking for a starting point for growth investing, the process is not very complicated. You have to look for and invest in companies that keep working to create new products and technology. Even though these companies have expensive stocks at this point in time, your investment will surely pay well in the long run.

GARP Investing

Now that you are familiar with the principles of both growth investing and value investing, let's explore the hybrid of these two stock selections called GARP or Growth at a Reasonable Price Investing.

As mentioned earlier GARP is a combination of value and growth investing. You should look for companies that are undervalued, but still have strong growth potential (i.e. value investing) as well as invest in companies a growth investor would invest in.

If you dig a little deeper, you'll see that GARP investors prefer companies that fall right between the criteria of value and growth investing. Because GARP borrows investment rules from both growth investing and value investing, people are still quite confused as to how this strategy works.

You might think that GARP investors have a portfolio with equal amounts of both value and growth stocks, but this is not the case. Just because GARP is a hybrid selection strategy, doesn't mean your portfolio should have equal number of growth and value stocks.

In case of GARP, investors identify and pick stocks on an individual basis. These stocks mostly are neither purely "growth" or "value" stocks, but a combination of the two.

Like growth investing, GARP investors are also interested in the growth potential of a company. Since there is no "magic formula" for predicting growth, GARP investors rely on their own judgment and interpretation of a company's performance. Another thing GARP investors focus their attention on is the ROE figure.

Income Investing

Income investing perhaps is the most straight forward stock picking strategy. If you are an income investor, you aim to pick companies that provide a steady stream of income. Most people confuse steady income with investing in fixed-income securities such as bonds; however, you can choose income investing and achieve a steady stream of income by investing in stocks that pay a solid dividend.

Generally, income investors prefer older and more established firms to achieve a steady income. If you invest in an older company that has already reached a certain size there will be a lesser chance to achieve high levels of growth. Plus, these companies are less likely to be in rapidly expanding industries. So, instead of reinvesting profits into their own growth, these established firms pay out dividends to their shareholders. Income investing is prominent in certain industries such as utility companies.

There are many good companies that pay great dividends but you need to calculate the dividend yield before investing your money. Remember, it is always better to invest in companies that give high dividend yields if you want to receive a steady and predictable stream of income over a long period of time.

Another important factor you need to keep in mind is the company's past dividend payout history. You need to determine whether or not the company can continue paying dividends before you make a final decision. Generally, if the company has been paying good dividends over long periods of time, the more likely it is to continue the same trend. Investing in companies that have a steady dividend record over the past 10, 15 and even 30 years is a good option.

Interestingly there are companies which increase their dividends every year, but you should not make your decision based solely on dividends. This is because higher dividends will result in lower retained earnings and problems could arise if the company has nothing to re-invest.

Being an income investor, you should analyze the company carefully before investing in it and buy only ones that have strong fundamentals. As we've discussed on a number of occasions, you can use your own interpretation and thinking to judge a "good company."

Another thing to remember is that investing in high dividend yield does not lower your risk, but you can actually minimize the risk associated with your investment by selecting solid companies.

CAN SLIM

CAN SLIM is another popular strategy of screening, buying and selling common stocks. The name does sound confusing, but it actually is a very successful investment strategy. Note: We'll only cover a brief introduction and here's a quick explanation of the seven important CAN SLIM factors:

1. **C - Current quarterly earnings per share**

You should choose stocks whose Earnings per Share (EPS) grow on a yearly basis and the percentage of growth must at least be 18-20%. The percentage of growth is a debatable feature but this investing system prefers nothing less than 18 to 20%. You can also assess the quality of EPS in other companies in the same industry. If most companies show solid earnings, you can say that the industry is thriving and the company is not a bad choice.

2. **A - Annual earnings per share**

The CAN SLIM system prefers that annual earnings per share figures of a company should show significant growth in each of the last five years. How much annual earnings growth is considered significant? Well, you can go for companies that have annual growth earnings in the range of 25 to 50%.

3. **N - New things**

The third important factor for a good company in the CAN SLIM system is that it must have undergone a change recently. This recent change can be anything ranging from new products or new management to changes in industry conditions. If a company has recently undergone a change, you should buy stocks when the prices start to hit high. It is very natural for novice investors to turn away from stocks that hit high prices because they fear that the company will only trade down from this level. But, the concept of CAN SLIM suggests that stocks that have just reached high prices, will continue the upward trend and reach even higher levels.

4. **S - Shares outstanding**

The "S" in CAN SLIM stands for demand and supply as well as shares outstanding. Outstanding shares technically are stocks held by investors and include shares that are owned by company's officers and insiders. Shares that are held by the public are also considered outstanding stock; however, shares that have been repurchased by the company do not belong in this category.

Because demand and supply of shares has a strong influence on the stock market, the company you want to invest in should have a small and reasonable number as outstanding shares. You can find this number on a company's balance sheet under the heading "Capital Stock".

Generally, CAN SLIM investors are not fond of investing in older companies with a large capitalization.

5. **L - Leaders**

This part of CAN SLIM analysis is very important. We know that every industry has market leaders and there are a number of market laggards as well. And, the key to success with CAN SLIM investing is how well you distinguish between market leaders and market laggards.

Make sure you always invest in companies that lead the market, and provide great gains to their shareholders. Try to stay away from those that lag behind as they'll only provide mediocre gains. Simply remember a golden rule. Identify strong contenders and always buy market leaders, not market laggards. Never let your emotions control your stock picking because if you pay more money for a market leader, you will be happy with your hard work in the end.

6. **I - Institutional sponsorship**

It is better to buy stocks that have at least 3 to 10 institutional sponsors. Plus these sponsors should have better-than-average performance in the recent past. Another important thing you need to remember is that companies that have excessive institutional ownership are not typically a good buy.

7. **M - General market**

As the name suggests, you need to recognize the direction in which your market is moving, i.e. bear or bull. Remember, the direction in which the market is moving determines whether you will win or lose. So, learn to figure out the market's overall current direction as well as interpret the general market indexes. This will help insure that you don't end up investing against the trend and lose significantly.

CAN SLIM is a great stock picking strategy because it incorporates winning tactics from all major investment strategies including fundamental, value, growth and technical analysis.

Dogs of the Dow

The "Dogs of the Dow" are 10 companies listed under the Dow Jones Industrial Average (DJIA) that have the highest dividend yield. This stock picking or investment strategy is popular because it is simple and quite successful as well.

If you use Dogs of the Dow strategy, you'll have to shuffle your portfolio and readjust it to fit these ten stocks equally. If this is the case, you might even have to get rid of three to four stocks every year and replace them with the remaining choices. One of the major reasons investors shuffle their portfolio is the fact that their stocks may have fallen out of the top 10 or might have been removed from the DJIA altogether.

Some of you may ask "is this strategy really so simple?" Well, all you have to do is reassess the 30 components of the DJIA at the end of every year. You can then easily figure out the ten stocks that have the highest dividend yield and create your portfolio based on each of these 10 stocks. It is better if your portfolio keeps the stocks as equally weighted as possible. You can hold onto these 10 stocks for one year and then reassess your portfolio to make larger gains.

Technical Analysis

Technical analysis is simply the opposite of fundamental analysis, something that we've been discussing in every stock picking method so far in this section. Technical analysts and investors are not really interested in the intrinsic value of a stock or any other fundamental factor. They only look at the trends shown by past data and charts and often technical investors make their money trading stocks of companies they know nothing about. Well, is this strategy a good move? The answer is pretty obvious, no. You can make short-term gains using this method, but it is not useful for long-term investment.

This sums up our discussion on picking the best stocks and the most well-known stock-picking strategies. Let's now see how you can set up a dividend portfolio.

Chapter 16
Setting up a Dividend Portfolio

16
Setting up a Dividend Portfolio

The phrase "knowledge is power" is perfect investment advice for every investor. You should be familiar with what are doing and most importantly, why you are doing it. Remember, if you don't know the rules, the investment game is going to be really tough. And, it is better if you stay away from action until you understand the game.

Since we are approaching the end of the Dividends Book, you might be thinking about building a portfolio for income. This particular section will give you some of the best tips for success, which means your portfolio will help you achieve your goals and fulfill your financial needs. Another important thing you need to remember is that there is no magical plan or shortcut. Even the best investors have achieved success with knowledge and patience.

As mentioned earlier, there is no shortcut for building a great portfolio and you need to spend time and analyze the market carefully. Things can get a little uncomfortable when the market is bearish as there are only a handful of valuable stocks at that point in time.

Even if you take a lot of time to find the winning stocks, there is nothing to worry about. What's better than investing your time in building a dividend portfolio that will give you high dividend yields!

Before you start your research, here's a simple tip you need to remember. Your safety comes first when building a portfolio. Just as you think clearly before making any financial decision, you need to be clear headed here as well. Make sure you set your goals and evaluate how much risk you can take before you start investing.

Once you are done with this step, start researching potential companies and buy stocks when the price is right. If you are not really convinced, you can wait a little longer as it is no use diving right into trouble. Remember, it is not simple to get rid of your investment so make sure you avoid unnecessary moves.

After you have decided your investments carefully, check whether or not it matches your plan. Plus, don't jump into high yield companies as they don't provide the income that you might be looking for. Remember, high yield companies are very tempting but there is a risk of a dividend cut.

How You Can Set Up Your Portfolio

Here are some more steps that will guide you in setting up your portfolio.

1. **Have At Least 8 To 10 Good Stocks.**

Remember, your portfolio is not a short-term solution and you are investing to secure your future. Make sure you put your money into 8 to 10 stocks and have a well-diversified portfolio. Focus more on receiving dividends and leave less-diversified portfolios for seasoned investors.

2. Diversify and Distribute Your Stocks Among Five to Seven Industries

Buying 10 to 15 stocks from the oil industry looks exciting but this is not a smart move. Remember, you can be badly affected if the majority of your stocks belong to the same industry sector. As mentioned earlier, dividend growth and stability is really important so try to buy leading stocks from different industries. This move will also protect you if any one industry is affected adversely.

3. Financial Stability is More Important than Simple Dividend Growth

While dividend growth is really helpful in achieving your financial goals, you need to focus more on financial stability. Try to go for stocks that are ranked in "As" by the Value Line Investment Survey, plus have a look at the company's credit ratings. Stocks ranked "A" have the lowest risk.

4. Find Companies that have a Long History of Raising Dividends

Make sure your portfolio has companies that have a long history of increasing their dividends every year. A good way to find such candidates is by looking through S&P's "Dividend Aristocrats" and Mergent's "Dividend Achievers". You may also have success in finding such companies by looking through the Value Line Investment Survey.

Remember, companies that have a long history of increasing their dividends over a long period of time have a better chance of doing well in the future.

5. Find Companies with Modest Payout Ratios

Don't forget to look at the payout ratio or Dividends as a Percentage of Earnings when buying stocks. Companies that have a payout ratio of 60% or less are the best.

6. Reinvest the Dividends

This little action can give surprising benefits. If you want to know how reinvesting dividends can help you, don't forget to refer back to the chapter on DRIPs.

7. Be patient and avoid making impulsive decisions.

Creating a portfolio is not all about catching every leading stock, but more about helping you to achieve your goals. Remember, if you are careful in a volatile environment, you are less likely to be negatively affected.

8. First Trust the Company Then Buy

You should only buy stocks of companies you trust, with the dividend yield coming second. Remember, you can only gain by investing in companies that have the ability to pay the listed dividend.

Chapter 17
Opening your own Account

17
Opening your own Account

An IRA can be opened through any reputable large financial institution, including banks, brokerage firms and mutual fund companies. Once you open an account, you will be offered a wide variety of investment options including CDs, mutual funds, stocks and bonds. You can then create a diversified retirement portfolio regardless of the IRA type you choose.

To set up your retirement account, first calculate your modified adjusted gross income (AGI) and figure out whether or not you are eligible for a Roth IRA. Don't forget to refer to chapter 3 to see if a Roth IRA is the best type of retirement account for you.

In addition to your modified adjusted gross income, you also need to have a close look at your contribution limits. Remember, Roth IRA accounts have an income limit and you cannot contribute more than your allowed limits.

After you have done your homework, you will need to decide on a firm to open your account with. There are many choices of brokerage firms, banks or other financial institutions to suit your needs. Scottrade.com and Etrade.

Dividends Book

com are well rated sites with plenty of online tools available for researching stocks.

Things you should consider when selecting your financial institution include:

1. Account fee and other charges. Make sure you know how much you have to pay annually and why.

2. Minimum required amount to open the account. Some brokers require you to deposit $600 to $2500.

3. Investment choices. You should select an institution that offers a wide variety of investment choices as well as detailed information about individual investments.

4. Many large institutions offer support tools such as online calculators, expert advice and market stats, so you can ask whether or not these services are offered by your firm.

5. Account funding options. The process of funding your account and transferring money should be hassle free.

Once you have decided your financial institution, you need to decide the type(s) of investments(s) you will purchase. If you go for a Roth IRA, you can buy any investment you like from the variety that is offered by your firm. However, you still need to do your research and find out which investments are right for you. If you've done your research, it is really easy to narrow down your choices when you have to make a final decision.

Dividends Book

We've discussed a number of investment options in this Book, and you should now be familiar with investments that have the most potential for growth. Stocks give you the best returns, but come with the most risk. Cash investment is less risky but it has the lowest rate of return.

The age at which you open an account is also important when considering your investment choices. You can afford to take more risk when you are young as you have more time to recover.

In addition to the steps mentioned above, you also need to determine whom you will name as beneficiary. Like any other financial account, you need to name a beneficiary who will inherit the account in case something happens to you. You will be given a form by your financial institution (brokerage firm or bank) to designate a beneficiary.

IRA accounts can be opened online and you can also open an account in person. The latter requires you to call for an appointment with your financial institution. If you wish to open the account online, simply visit the broker or bank website and follow their instructions.

The two companies I prefer to use are Scott Trade, which has offices nationwide, and online at www.Scottrade.com and E*Trade online at www.Etrade.com. Scott Trade offers classes in person at their offices, and classes online. Scottrade has discount trades if done online, and they offer discount trades if you wish to trade in person or by phone. E*trade has offices as well and offers similar services.

Dividends Book

Make sure you have the following information when opening your account.

1. Your social security number as well as the social security number of your beneficiary.

2. The account number of your current institution if transferring funds.

3. Your salary information. This is required to determine your eligibility for a Roth IRA.

Once you have opened an account, follow your financial institution instructions for making contributions to your account. Don't forget to keep track of the yearly limits to a Roth IRA.

This brings us to the end of the Dividends Book. Here's hoping that you make the best investment decisions based on the ideas and guidelines mentioned here. Remember, you make significant gains when you make smart decisions and the Dividends Book helps you do just that. For more information and advice on investment options, feel free to visit www.DividendDetective.com He has some of the best dividend research out there. If you like to do your own research you can go to yahoo finance, and google finance where they both have dividend stock screeners based on the parameters you key in the program. For the latest updates and information on Dividends, you can visit our website www.DividendsBook.com

Dividends Book

Thank you for reading my book, and here's to your success with Dividends.

As My Dad always says, how can you argue with the success of our countries Richest Families in preserving and growing their wealth with Dividends?

www.ingramcontent.com/pod-product-compliance
Lightning Source LLC
Chambersburg PA
CBHW071757200526
45167CB00017B/400